Mindful Money

DISCLAIMER

The ideas, concepts and everything else in this book are simply my opinions based on what has worked for me and what I've learned from being bitten in the behind. This book summarises the lessons of my journey to date. They may not continue to work for me, and they may not work for you.

While I hope that this book will provide you with some valuable guidance, I cannot possibly know the full details of any reader's personal situation or needs. As the author, I make no representations as to the accuracy, completeness, currentness, suitability or validity of any information in this book. I will not be liable for any errors or omissions. While I have gone to every effort to research everything in this creation, all information provided was up to date as of the date of publication. As with everything in life, you are responsible for your own choices. There are no guarantees here or in life. I wish you the best on your journey.

Mindful Money

More Money, More Freedom, More Happiness

KEL GALAVAN

ORPEN PRESS

Published by
Orpen Press
Upper Floor, Unit B3
Hume Centre
Hume Avenue
Park West Industrial Estate
Dublin 12

email: info@orpenpress.com
www.orpenpress.com

Paperback ISBN 978-1-78605-122-6
ePub ISBN 978-1-78605-123-3

Printed in Dublin by SPRINTprint Ltd

This book is dedicated to my husband, Dave, who supports me in everything I do, even when none of it makes sense to him. This book is also dedicated to my children, Ria and Aaron; they are the reason it was written and my driving force. I love you all so much.

ACKNOWLEDGEMENTS

I am an avid reader. I usually have several on the go at any one time. As such, I have read the acknowledgements page of many books. The cynic inside often scoffing; sure, there may have been some people who helped smooth out parts here and there, but really it was the author who did the heavy lifting. Then I wrote this book.

Editing

Mindful Money would not exist without my editor, Eileen O'Brien from Orpen Press; her level-headedness, encouragement, persistence and faith in me dragged me across the finish line. Everyone on the team rowed in to get this work across the line. I was fortunate to see behind the curtain of what it takes to get a book from manuscript to the shelf. The experience was incredible, fun and showed me what real dedication looks like.

Remarkably, she's still speaking to me.

Cover and author photos

Rachael Taylor Fawsitt (www.rachaelvictoria.ie), whom I met through www.creators.ie, where all us Irish bloggers hang out. Rachael was the first person ever to take professional photos of me. It was through watching her work and how she crafted the shots that I came to realise what a creative skill it is. She not only has the ability to capture who I am on camera, but she even managed to make me look presentable, something my mother lamented over for years.

When it comes to photography, let's just say I'm missing the gene on that one. However, I have Rachael and her talents to lean into, thank goodness.

To you

And to all the readers of www.mrssmartmoney.com and @mrssmartmoneyhq on Instagram. Your questions and comments through it all have helped me more fully understand what those aspiring to build a better life for their loved ones want and need to know.

The energy, enthusiasm and goodwill that are present to better ourselves, grow and learn have been the most humbling and energising experience of my life.

Thank you.

PREFACE

I turned 40 just as the Covid-19 lockdown commenced in March 2020. It was a birthday to remember, but not for the reasons I had planned. It was a chilly spring day, yet warm enough to hint that summer was on its way. The kids had been sent home from school just a few days before, with what turned out to be the futile hope that they would be returning two weeks later.

I sat in the garden listening to the airwaves filled with talk of coronavirus and rising death tolls. Talk of the recession and global collapse were sprinkled throughout, juxtaposed with the crisp morning. The world as we knew it was changing beyond recognition; there was not a thing we could do except stay in our homes and stay safe. I turned off the radio, preferring to sit in silence.

I knew there and then that I needed to hone in on what I did best. I needed to tune out distractions and focus on what I could control. So I drew on my experience from the No-Spend Year and applied the lessons I had learned. I had already submitted the manuscript of *The No-Spend Year*, to my publisher. This first iteration was designed and written before the Covid-19 pandemic flooded across our world. It was penned at a time when most people were living at breakneck speed, going through commuter hell, when work–life balance seemed more like a fairytale than a reality. However, in this strange new unfolding world, I knew I could do more. I knew that this book could be more useful, more impactful and more life-changing for those looking to refocus their life after Covid forced them to pause it.

The No-Spend Year had arisen from my need to create a better work–life balance. I felt that my children's childhood was passing me by, and I wasn't around to see it. So, after much deliberation, I finally decided to step back from my 16-year career to spend more time with them. To do so meant that I would be cutting our income in half. If I was going to do that, I was going to make sure that that income worked as hard as it possibly could for us. I knew there had to be a better way – there had to be a way to get our money to work for us, to live a great life now while still building a solid future. This was the inception of the No-Spend Year of 2019. A year where I stopped dyeing my hair and gave up alcohol, takeaways and eating out. It was the year I banned buying clothes, embraced minimalism and cut our food budget in half. It was also the year that changed the trajectory of my family's life in a way I would have never imagined. It was the best thing ever to happen to my family and me.

So with Covid-19 invading our world, I tasked myself with transforming the learnings from the No-Spend Year into a book that could transcend almost all economic times. The lessons passed on in these pages are the lessons that got me through not only the No-Spend Year, but the pandemic too. They are what I will continue to live by, as they freed me from the fear of uncertainty. They are the habits that allowed me to transition to a life I love; they are also the habits that kept the ship steady as we navigated this brave new world. I no longer fear the future. I command the direction of my own and my family's life, and that feels fantastic.

TABLE OF CONTENTS

INTRODUCTION

This is the story of how we irrevocably changed our lives. It is the story of a pivot in a career, a transformation in lifestyle made possible by the power of mindful money. This book has the potential to change your life too. I know this because the habits detailed in these pages changed ours. There is power in doing the small things well. The No-Spend Year was proof of that for me, and our new life is the result. I will share everything that I've learned; nothing will be left out.

Mindful money can ensure that whatever the economy throws at you, whatever state the world is in, you have the resources and peace of mind to weather it as best possible. I want to give you the power to control your own path, to provide you with the breathing space to figure out what you want from life and make the choices that will get you there.

However, this power does not come for free – you must understand the knowledge within and act on it. Embrace the habits with vigour to see the magic unfold. This book will teach the skills; it is up to you to adapt them to your life. Money treated well will protect you in hard times and build for you in good times. You are not its slave, you are its master. And once you decide to take control and not be controlled, that is where freedom is found.

Part I

THE BIG PICTURE

1

IRELAND'S CREDIT HISTORY CHECK

It is not far back in our history that Ireland had nothing, that every item was precious, and anything new was hard-won. Credit didn't exist, and much of the population lived hand to mouth. The end of this time in our history was marked by the crippling recession of the 1980s.[1] Mortgage interest rates hit highs of 16.25 per cent.[2] Ireland was a poor country by Western European standards, with high rates of poverty, unemployment and inflation and low economic growth. Women were mainly homemakers.[3]

Then the Celtic Tiger arrived in the early 1990s, catapulting us forward at unprecedented speed. Money rushed in from Europe and elsewhere. Credit became freer, products flooded our shelves, and we raced to borrow and buy. Businesses and industry flourished. We welcomed the arrival of hundreds of new companies and well-paid jobs. We had finally arrived.[4]

We had a perfect storm for rapid growth. Our educational system started pumping out huge numbers of highly qualified graduates, 60 per cent more in Ireland than in the rest of Europe, to be exact. Mass immigration resulted from the return of our experienced overseas counterparts, who had left in the 1980s in search of a better life. Thanks to the lifting of the marriage ban in the 1970s, the first generation of women to be educated and have a full career path ahead of them entered the workforce. During these years the Irish workforce grew almost five times faster than in the rest of Europe.[5]

THE CELTIC TIGER ROARS, BUT NOT FOR LONG

Finally, we were catching up to some of our more affluent neighbours, and boy did we put on a show. In those years, we grew at a rate faster than any economy in history that I'm aware of. Ireland expanded at a rate of 9.4 per cent between 1995 and 2000. This growth continued at an average of 5.9 per cent during the following decade.[6] The excitement of having spending power for the first time in our history was palpable. House prices rose through the roof, as did the cost of living. Credit became normalised, and banks issued it like candy. Mortgages that were 100 per cent were not uncommon, and we ate it up.[7] We rushed out and bought everything we couldn't afford with the newfound wealth we didn't know how to manage and credit we didn't understand.

By 2007, we were riding a wave of generous salaries and lavish lifestyles. This time we had outraced all of Europe, to the point where our per capita purchasing power in terms of our national output was about 10 per cent higher than in the rest of Western Europe.[8] Mortgage interest rates hovered around 5.15 per cent. However, these good times could not last. The bubble burst in the property market. A tsunami of debt roared through the whole economy. We were crushed under the pressure.

By 2012, house prices were below 2001 levels. All the gains made during the Celtic Tiger years had been erased.[9] Unemployment rose from 4.2 per cent in 2007 to 14.6 per cent in 2012. The Central Statistics Office (CSO) estimated that 34,500 people left the country between 2009 and 2010, the most substantial net emigration since 1989. Ireland was overwhelmed by emergency budgets, toxic banks, job losses, negative equity and strikes. Banks threatened insolvency as the fear of losing savings on deposits caused a run on more than one. People queued for hours to withdraw their life savings, not knowing if they would ever see the money.[10] In response, the government issued a 2-year unlimited guarantee of all debt (the Credit Institutions Financial Stabilisation Act, or CIFS guarantee) in September 2008. This move, also known as the bank guarantee, did its job and tempered the crippling anxiety felt across society. NAMA was created in 2009 to take custody of some of the larger property bank loans, which eased the burden on the banks and kept them afloat.[11]

Ireland was in over its head and knew it needed support. The so-called European troika, the decision group formed by the European Commission (EC), the European Central Bank (ECB) and the International Monetary Fund (IMF), stepped in and signed the Economic Adjustment Programme for Ireland in December 2010. This agreement, more commonly referred to as the Bailout programme, gave a total of €85 billion in financial support to Ireland.[12] The programme was the key to Ireland finally getting back on its feet. Unfortunately, it came at a very high price. It left the people of Ireland carrying the burden of this debt while piecing their own lives back together.

It took years, but by 2018 we were finally getting our country's debt to a more manageable level.[13] Then 2019 rolled around. Average annual earnings had risen to higher than the pre-crisis income[14] and Ireland was very much on the recovery end of the recession. A small ray of hope shone across the economy. There was a spring in the Irish population's step as we headed into 2020. A year that will be embedded in our memory in ways we never could have predicted.

RECOVERY POWER

Even with the significant strides made in the preceding years, Ireland's national debt was hovering at just over €200 billion facing into the pandemic. On a per capita basis, that was the third-highest in the world, eclipsed only by the US and Japan. This equated €42,000 for every man, woman and child in the state. Having such massive debt leaves the state exposed and vulnerable in the event of another global downturn. By October 2020 this had risen to €223.6 billion according to the central bank with more borrowings in the pipeline.

The Covid-19 pandemic caused a dramatic slowdown in the economy. We have been thrown into another crisis before we've adequately freed ourselves from the last. All key sectors of the economy are now heavily indebted, including households and industry. Despite low interest rates, Ireland's repayments on its debt are relatively high. In 2018, Ireland's interest payments were 6.4 per cent of government revenue. This was the fourth-highest in the EU. Ireland is still breaking its own records.[15]

Ireland is not alone when it comes to debt burdens. The world is seeing global and historical highs of debt since the pandemic. Governments around the world owe $188 trillion, which is 230 per cent of global output. So it is not just Ireland breaking records, everyones looking for a shot at the title. Debt level records seem to be broken daily, and there is no blueprint for what will happen next.[16]

HAVE WE LEARNED ANYTHING?

In 2020, the government was put in an impossible position: it had to borrow to keep the country afloat, as it did not have a Rainy-Day Fund to fall back on. It was forced to borrow more on top of its already heavy debt burden. In light of the recent upheaval, have we learned our lesson on the dangers of too much borrowing? Did we learn any lessons from the housing debt crisis, only a decade ago? Has our recent turbulent past been enough to make us learn?

It appears not. According to the CSO, in addition to the government drowning in debt, we seem to be doing the same individually. In terms of household debt, the total value amounts to €136.9 billion or around €28,000 per person in 2019. The growth rate on consumer credit was 5.6 per cent as of August 2019. Loan terms of 1 to 5 years represent two-thirds of lending, and these tend for the most part to be short-term personal loans.[17] A 2018 report on the whole State of Ireland stated that 26.1 per cent have a mortgage on their main property, 30.4 per cent have non-mortgage loans, 7.9 per cent have an overdraft and 12.7 per cent have credit card debt. With a total of 51.8 per cent of the Irish population carrying some form of debt, it appears that the danger of the credit crisis is a distant memory already. We are still borrowing as fast as we can.[18]

The amount of debt carried varies widely between demographics, with the over-65s carrying the least amount of debt, at 13.9 per cent. This rises dramatically in households with children. Of these young families, 49.1 per cent have mortgages and, more worryingly, 41.5 per cent have non-mortgage loans, 9.4 per cent have overdrafts and 21.9 per cent have credit card debt. In total, an eye-watering 74.3 per cent of households with children are carrying debt. That's almost three-quarters of all young families burdened with several forms of mortgages, personal loans, car loans and consumer credit card debt at the same time. Families with children appear to be laden with the lion's share of household debt. At what is one of the most expensive times in life, these same parents are indenturing their futures for most of their working lives. There has to be a better way.

WHAT ARE WE SPENDING OUR MONEY ON?

In a 2018 CSO spending report, four out of ten households reported that their regular expenses were less than their income. This means that only 40 per cent of Irish people are living within their means, i.e. only 40 per cent of people are saving. This leaves the majority of 60 per cent spending more than they are earning every month.[19] Saving money, building deposits, paying down debt or striving for a secure future is an impossible task unless a person is living below their means.

'But life is so expensive', I hear you cry, 'Making ends meet is so hard', wail others. Yes indeed, we are not a cheap country to live in. However, how we spend our money as a nation could be improved. In 1980, the largest proportion of total household expenditure related to food, at 27.7 per cent. However, by 2015-2016 this had fallen to 14.7 per cent. Conversely, the percentage of spending on housing increased from 7.2 per cent in 1980 to 19.6 per cent in 2015-2016. The proportion of total food expenditure has shown a steady decline over the past 35 years, whereas most of the house price increases occurred during the short period between 1999 and 2016.

House prices and food are two significant expenses that most of us cannot avoid. However, our increased buying power and rapid growth economy have changed how we spend the discretionary portion of our income, specifically when it comes to miscellaneous goods. The proportion of expenditure on various products, services and other expenses increased from 20.5 per cent to 33.6 per cent over that same thirty-five-year period. This percentage is reflected right across all incomes, demographics and geographical locations in Ireland.[20] We are all guilty of this increased spending. Since food, transportation, housing, clothes, household goods, fuel and light are not included in this number, miscellaneous goods can easily be categorised as non-essential spending or, as I refer to it, wants and not needs: things like eating out, socialising, gadgets, homewares and holidays. Irrespective of income, we just can't seem to live within our means. A third of our money is spent on unnecessary things, which shows that saving, for the most part, is not an income problem. It is a spending problem.

2

WHAT'S NORMAL
IS NOT ALWAYS GOOD

Debt has been normalised. Debt has become so routine that carrying several forms of it at any one time has become a socially acceptable way of being. Being the proud owner of a mortgage, car loan, personal loan, credit card debt and an overdraft concurrently is seen as an acceptable way to be. However, the normalisation of something does not make it right.

SMOKING IS GOOD FOR YOU

Between the 1920s and early 1950s, advertising slogans made health claims to promote smoking. Taglines included statements like, 'More Doctors smoke Camels than any other cigarettes'. One advertisement featured an infant and the words, 'Before you scold me, Mom ... maybe you should light up a Marlboro'. Another newspaper ad featured a kindly dentist and the phrase, 'Viceroys filter the Smoke! As your Dentist I would recommend Viceroys'. These advertisements were commonplace until 1953, when health concerns became overwhelming, and the link to cancer indisputable.[21] While tobacco does have a sedative effect, any benefits are far outweighed by its addictive and carcinogenic properties.

'THE RADIUM WATER WORKED FINE UNTIL HIS JAW FELL OFF'

Radium, when first discovered, was little understood. All that was known was that it gave off energy. Energy was a good thing and it was deduced that adding some of this energy to the body couldn't do any harm – in fact, it probably had lots of benefits, right? This assumption resulted in a range of health and beauty products being launched with claims they would increase vitality and give a healthy glow.[22] Products containing radium were prescribed for any ailment where a lack of energy was the root cause.[23]

A product by the name of Radithor (radium dissolved in water) was commonly prescribed to help heal broken bones and increase energy levels. Eben Byers, an American socialite and champion golfer, became notorious for drinking several bottles a day. Until he withered away at the age of 51 in 1932, that was. The headline of the *Wall Street Journal* story about his death read, 'The radium water worked fine until his jaw fell off.'[24,25]

At the height of radium's popularity, another use for it became normal. The element gave a luminescent glow that made it possible to read watches in the dark without the need for batteries. Young women were hired in factories around the world to hand-paint clock digits using radium paint mixed on-site, and trained in a technique of licking the end of the brushes to ensure an excellent, pointed brush. It allowed for accuracy and speed – both positives for the girls, who were paid by the piece. This practice was taught in training and widely encouraged. The air was full of radium dust as the paint was mixed on-site. The girls would wear their best dresses to work, allowing the radium to cling to skin and clothes, and would literally be glowing when they went to the speakeasy after work. Soon, many of these women developed bone cancers and the majority developed radium-caused tumours, with over half of them dying within years of exposure.[26] Far from being a panacea, radium was deadly when used incorrectly.

Radium has many uses in medicine, both for treating cancer patients and in industrial radiography. It has helped save many lives and made parts of industry possible. However, these benefits were only discovered after much research, due diligence and great tragedy.

These are a couple of examples to illustrate that not everything we as a society embrace as standard is in our best interest. How we choose to use a tool like radium, cigarettes or credit can make or break us.

CREDIT NEEDS TO BE USED WITH CARE

While I am not saying that credit is identical to tobacco or radium, what I want to do is illustrate that just because something has been adopted as normal and its great benefits have been touted, that does not mean that it will benefit everyone. There are many pitfalls to using credit and carrying debt, so care needs to be taken when considering it. It can be a millstone around your neck or it can be the key to a great life. Unfortunately, using credit is one of those things we can rush into without thinking. Once it gets a hold, many spend the rest of their lives trying to get free of it. Having credit freely available is a good thing when used in the right way. However, wielded incorrectly can set us back decades and even ruin lives.

These examples are not to keep you up at night or scare you into locking the door and never trying anything new ever again. They are to illustrate that we, individually and as a society, don't always get things right. Sometimes, mistakes slip through that can do great damage. Neither I am saying that a life without any debt is the best way to be. However, just because something is available and socially accepted does not mean that it is the best path. Ask any lemming who just leapt off the cliff if they have any second thoughts on following the crowd.

3

HOW THE ECONOMY WORKS

O ur past – and most likely our future – is littered with booms and busts. It has been like this from time immemorial. But why does this happen with such dramatic regularly? How can we not seem to stop these cycles that are forever throwing us off our stride, causing so much damage as they unfold? Understanding how an economy works is vital to understanding these peaks and troughs. Once you know, preparing for them becomes much easier.

An economy is simply the sum of all the transactions that take place in a given place. Transactions consist of a buyer, who spends money, and a seller, who provides a product or service for that money. One person's spending is another person's income. In a cash-only society, a person can only buy things with cash they have earned, usually through working. If a person does not work, they do not get paid and therefore cannot purchase a product or service. This type of economy cannot have highs and lows because each transaction made is paid in full at the time of purchase. As a concept, this is ideal, as no one ever owes anything, and everyone gets paid. However, only being able to use the money you already have can make it very difficult for the average person to make larger purchases, like a house or car.

This is where credit comes in. Credit is spent just like money. If credit is available to a person, their buying power shoots up, allowing them to afford things they would not otherwise be able to buy. This is good, as it enables people to buy homes and start businesses. Credit is a large part of the money we spend today, but is poorly understood. Credit acts as money, but it is not money.

Credit is tricky because it has many names and comes in many forms. As soon as credit is created, it turns into debt. This debt does different things. It is income to the lender and an expense to the borrower. Lenders want to lend money to make a profit and buyers want to buy something that they can't afford. Credit helps both lenders and borrowers get what they want. In a perfect world, when everything is working as it should be, the debt is paid back with interest and the loan is settled. Everyone is happy.

A good example is the house-buying process. We save a deposit and fill out all the proper forms until a lender, usually a bank, deems us creditworthy enough to lend us the mortgage required for the house our little hearts are set on. This credit approval dramatically increases our ability to buy. It allows us to purchase more than we otherwise could. However, by making this one massive purchase on credit, we are indentured to banks for decades because of the debt repayments with interest that we must make. We promise large chunks of our future earnings to make up for the one-off big spend. To pay this money back, we must spend less on other things for that long period to afford those repayments. Overall, a mortgage is considered 'good debt'. A car could potentially also be included here, as it may be the only way to get you to your job, the job that creates the income you need to live. However, there is a vast difference between buying a good enough car versus a brand-new lifestyle car that makes a statement and is far more than you need to get you to and from work.

The other side of the debt coin is 'bad debt'. This is when credit is used to fund a lifestyle: buying a new TV, eating out, clothes, holidays and gadgets. If these things are bought on credit because we can't afford them now, it means that we are living beyond our means. These are all depreciating assets that do not generate a return. If they are bought using credit, they are a drain on resources and never give back, unlike a home or a car. This level of spending may appear sustainable if all goes well and the debt is paid back as agreed. If this happens, the transaction disappears, and the world goes on in an upward trajectory.

However, a change in circumstance, like a job loss or economic dip, can cause a default on the debt. That debt, just like real cash, is someone else's income. Just like every time you spend money, you are creating revenue for the receiver of that money. If you can't pay, then others don't get paid. If this happens on a large scale, a crash, dip, or recession can be triggered, just as it was in 2008 because much of the housing market was bought on credit. Once the dominoes began to topple, the actual level of debt became real, and the economy took a nosedive because no one could pay anyone else.

This is why credit, not cash, causes peaks and troughs in economies. Without credit, there would not have been a bubble to burst.

Credit is not always bad, and finding a balance is vital. It is useful when it can increase buying power for assets like a home to live in, or a car or laptop that allows you to create income. Using credit with care, only taking it on when absolutely necessary, and carrying as little as possible, allows you to weather economic changes or big surprises in life better.

4

WHAT IS MONEY ANYWAY?

What is money? In times past, there was no currency. People bartered with each other to get what they needed. Trading chicken for grain or cows for building materials was the usual practice. This bartering worked well for the most part until someone wanted to trade but had nothing that the seller needed. If a chicken farmer needed leather, but the leather trader had no use for chicken, striking an agreement was difficult. A universally accepted unit of trade was required, but what could that unit be?

WHERE MONEY BEGAN

There is a tiny island in the middle of the Pacific Ocean called Yap that is famous because it answers the fundamental question, 'What is money?' Hundreds of years ago its inhabitants came up with an unusual form of money. The Yap didn't have gold or any other precious metals; instead, they used coins made from stone. Some were the size of cars, up to four metres in diameter. These massive stone discs were made of calcite, a type of bright, crystalline limestone, that is quite stunning. In the sunlight, they can almost blind you. The important thing here is that the people of Yap at some stage decided that they needed something to store value. They needed something they could use to pay for things. But it had to be something that everyone in society agreed was valuable. Like many societies, the people of Yap chose objects they found beautiful, in the same way that other societies chose gold. So they chose these beautiful glowing white stones called Rai.

Explorers from Yap found huge calcite caves hundreds of kilometres away. They carved the calcite into massive discs and somehow managed to carry them back home in bamboo canoes. As boats got better, they were able to take bigger stones. Some of the Rais found on the island were several metric tonnes in weight, the weight of two small cars.

Within Yap society, a piece of this stone was treasured and reserved for big purchases in life, not day-to-day spending. Examples of this include dowries, or insurance in case a crop failed and they were exchanged for food. These stones were a concrete form of money and not easy to exchange at all. So it is not surprising that more convenient ways of exchanging money were adopted as time went on. Instead of physically moving the cumbersome rocks – which could weigh up to 2000 kilograms – from person to person, they moved on to a more abstract system. The Rai no longer had to physically change hands. Instead, agreements were struck for the rocks to change ownership while remaining in situ. Most of the contracts were verbal and became part of the tribe's oral lore. There is even an unusually large stone that fell from a boat off the coast of Yap decades ago. No one has ever seen it since it dropped, but it is owned, has value and changes ownership when exchanged for something else. The islanders still use the stones as a form of currency, though they have also incorporated a more convenient currency, the dollar.[27]

These Rai stones in the Yap community may seem strange and almost comical to us at first; however, we also use 'stone money' all the time. A check is a promise of a money transaction, but no real money changes hands. If one person uses PayPal to pay a friend, no money changes hands. Instead, we trust that we will receive the money. Trust is a massive part of why our modern financial system works.

THE ROLE OF GOLD

Yap is an excellent example of how the concept of currency developed. However, for the so-called fiat currencies, extra steps were necessary to reach the same level of trust in integrity. A fiat currency is one issued by a government that is not backed by gold or any other commodity. It stands alone. Fiat currencies do not have intrinsic value, unlike gold which has value in addition to its cost per gram. Gold can be used in manufacturing, jewellery, dentistry, and mobile phones, to name a few. Government-issued currency or fiat currency does not have this added value: the note itself is worthless. Instead, we as a community agree to believe in the amount printed on that note. As long as this trust is intact, money has value.

Through the end of the nineteenth century into the first half of the twentieth century, many of the world's most powerful countries – the USA, Britain, Japan, and European countries – adopted the gold standard. The gold standard was the monetary unit associated with the value of gold coins in circulation. This worked well, as gold was solid, real and easy to understand. However, gold is heavy and not convenient to carry around in large amounts. So to make gold more practical, gold-backed banknotes were put in circulation, and so began the spread of paper money, or banknotes. The aim of these notes was to replace gold in day-to-day transactions. This was called the gold standard. The gold standard was a system in which gold coins themselves did not circulate. Instead, governments agreed to sell gold bullion on demand at a fixed price in exchange for the circulating currency. At any stage, anyone could walk into a bank and request to swap their paper money for gold coins. The gold standard fixed the exchange rates between currencies, preventing them from fluctuating. This set exchange rate with the gold standard enabled the widespread use of paper money. Even though paper notes did not have intrinsic value, they were backed by the promise of being worth a set amount of gold. Safe in this knowledge, countries built trust between each other and trade agreements grew.[28]

The gold standard remained in place until the signing of the Bretton Woods Agreement in New Hampshire in the USA in July 1944. The Bretton Woods Agreement set up a system of rules, institutions, and procedures to regulate international monetary policy. The International Monetary Fund (IMF) and the International Bank for Reconstruction and Development (IBRD), which today is part of the World Bank Group, came into being. The United States, which controlled two-thirds of the world's gold, insisted the Bretton Woods system would consist of both gold and the US dollar. This agreement made the dollar the world reserve currency, alongside gold.

The Bretton Woods agreement stayed in place until 1971, when the United States, under President Nixon, unilaterally severed the link between the dollar and gold, effectively bringing the Bretton Woods system to an end and rendering the dollar a fiat currency. This, for the first time, allowed the USA to print money without having gold to back it. Without the limitations of gold, America could print as much money as it needed to reduce its debts after the war.[29] At the same time, many fixed currencies, including the pound sterling, also became free-floating or fiat currencies by breaking their link with gold. As a result, no currency is directly linked with gold anymore, leaving each banknote to rely solely on society to trust its value[30], just like the people of Yap trusted in their Rai stones.

In Money We Trust

Unfortunately, throughout history, this trust has been broken more than once. In 2016 the Indian government announced that existing 500- and 1000-rupee notes were worthless; these notes accounted for 86 per cent of the country's cash supply. New notes would be issued through bank accounts to anyone who opened one. The action aimed to curtail the shadow economy and reduce the use of illicit and counterfeit cash to fund illegal activity. The announcement was followed by prolonged cash shortages, creating significant disruption throughout the country. People seeking to trade in their banknotes had to stand in lengthy queues, and several deaths were linked to the rush to exchange cash.[31]

In 2015, the Zimbabwean government demonetised the Zimbabwean dollar, rendering it worthless. Hyperinflation was running at 500 billion per cent. The government eventually agreed to credit $5 US dollars to bank accounts with balances of up to $175 quadrillion Zimbabwean dollars. An account with more than that received $1 US dollar for every $35 quadrillion Zimbabwean dollars above the $175 quadrillion Zimbabwean dollars. The aim of this move was to stabilise the economy and the Zimbabwean dollar was erased from the country's financial system in favour of the US dollar as the country's legal tender.[32,33]

Another example of demonetisation, albeit less dramatic, occurred when the nations that were part of the European Economic and Monetary Union adopted the euro in 2002. To switch to the euro, authorities first fixed exchange rates for the various national currencies. The Irish punt exchange rate was fixed as €1.27.[34] The introduction of the euro demonetised the existing EU currencies, meaning they were no longer legal tender. The old monies remained convertible into euros for a certain period to allow a smooth transition through demonetisation. It is still possible to exchange old Irish punts for euros at the Central Bank today.[35]

Currency is a fickle and changeable thing, which is why it is essential to understand that money is nothing more than a tool to fulfil a purpose. Money is what we, as a society, want it to be and trust it to be. It is up to you to take advantage of this tool, see it for the life-building thing that it can be. Make it work for you and not against you. The more a person understands money, the greater power they possess and the more proficient they will become at wielding it. Money does not have emotions or wants. It is simply a means to an end – to your ends, if you choose to make it so.

PART II

GROUNDING

5

LET'S GET SOME BASICS STRAIGHT

When it comes to money, there are a few basics that need to be grasped to put everything you have just read into context. Once these concepts are understood, creating new mindful spending habits will not only make sense but will be the natural next step.

AFFLUENCE VS WEALTH

Affluence and wealth are often used interchangeably. In truth, they could not be more different. An affluent person looks well-to-do but regularly spends up to and beyond their income to maintain that lifestyle. A wealthy person may or may not display wealth externally but has assets built up to a point where they can choose to work or not to maintain the lifestyle that they have.

An affluent person can fall prey to the temptation to spend beyond their income, resulting in credit being used to get to the end of the month. Purchases like holidays, clothes and entertainment are prioritised over saving and investing. Depreciating assets are bought that lose value and do not give a return. Most of us might not feel that we live an affluent lifestyle, but if you find that you are buying things on impulse – things like that cute handbag, a meal out or another pair of blue jeans to add to the ten pairs you already have, while leaning on credit to do so – that is the hallmark of affluence.

Unfortunately, affluence can be a dangerous mistress. An affluent life-style may seem acceptable when there is income and the economy is stable. However, if that revenue stream is turned off through a job loss, pay cut or downturn, then the affluent lifestyle is at risk of coming to a sharp and jagged halt. This has been borne out in recession after recession. With every up, there is a down. If a portion of income is not saved, and loans are taken out for personal spending, those debt payments cannot be met when there is a loss of income, and then the spiral of default, repossession, and the crushing weight of affluence come crashing down.

Wealth, on the other hand, has less to do with material belongings and more to do with having enough money saved up. Real wealth is where enough passive income is generated so that a job is not needed to maintain a preferred lifestyle. Another way of looking at wealth is this: if your primary source of income was lost, how long could you maintain your current life before you ran into trouble? What savings, pensions and assets could you lean on if things went wrong, and how long would these resources last? The longer this period of time, the higher your protection against change, and the wealthier you are.

Focusing on growing wealthy does not mean you cannot own and enjoy beautiful things. It implies that beautiful things should only be considered after the basics of saving have been taken care of. I could buy that fantastic pair of shoes in the excellent sale and look the part of a rich woman. Alternatively, I could save and invest that money and actually grow to be that wealthy woman and only then buy as many pairs of shoes as I please.

INCOME VS NET WORTH

We are all guilty of falling into the clutches of affluence now and again; we are human, after all. The key here is to understand the difference: income does not equal wealth, it is the amount of income that we keep that is the key to wealth. Understanding this difference has an impact on how money is treated. And if it is treated mindfully, it can grow.

Have you ever had a conversation where someone kept mentioning their five- or six-figure income? It is a a badge of honour for many affluent people. However, if you pick up a magazine and read the latest about the ultra-wealthy, the article is rarely about their income. Affluence is measured in earnings; wealth, on the other hand, is calculated in terms of net worth. Income doesn't matter if net worth is not building in the background. Living below your means allows for savings to be made and ensures success over time.

Someone who earns €35,000 a year and can live off €30,000 is substantially better off than someone earning €130,000 a year who needs €131,000 to live. How much you make does not determine how much you have and how much you have does not dictate how much you need. Mindful spending gears your life towards the path of increasing your net worth. Living below your means is within your control, and it is within this control that real life-changing money is nurtured.

NUMBERS HAVE IMPLICATIONS

The words million, billion and trillion are regularly and flippantly bandied about like they are all from the same family of numbers. They are not. In recent times, countries seem to be borrowing trillions just as they would billions like there is no difference. However, these three levels of money are worlds apart. An excellent way to illustrate this is to use the analogy of time. Time is relatable. It is something that we can comprehend and measure. How long ago would you guess a million seconds ago was? Go on have a guess, take a moment and throw out a number.

Okay, I won't keep you in suspense. A million seconds ago would be almost 12 days ago. With that number in your mind, how long ago do you think a billion seconds might be? A million and a billion are close enough, don't you think? However, my dear reader, a billion seconds ago would bring you back almost 32 years. Not 12 days, but 32 years. Now moving onto the big one, the trillion-second timeline. How long ago might you guess that would fall? Fifty, a hundred or maybe a thousand years ago? Not even close, a trillion seconds ago was just about 32,000 years ago. Take a moment to think those numbers over.[36]

To be a millionaire is something that many of us strive for. It is something that is so far from our current reality that it seems like a near impossible target. Yet, when we look at the debt of our country or the world, these numbers take on astronomical proportions. It illustrates the significant disparity between these often-interchanged words. Once you know the real value of each, it gives a bit of perspective on the sums that we as a country, a continent and a globe need to pay back.

6

DO NOT UNDERESTIMATE THE ROLE OF CHANCE IN YOUR LIFE

Don't underestimate the role of chance in your life. It is easy to assume that diligence and hard work will always work in your favour and that things will work out. It is easy to assume that wealth and poverty are a result of the choices we make. Underestimating the role of chance and luck in our lives is easier still. The 2008 recession and the more recent Covid-19 pandemic are excellent reminders of this. We cannot control most of the world we live in. Instead, we need to play the hand we are dealt. No path to money and freedom is built on a straight line.

Never underestimate the power that the influence of family, culture and country we are born into and the impact that they have on our life path and the choices that we make. They combine to play a more prominent role than we care to admit. While it is essential to believe in the value of hard work, it is vital to understand that not everyone began from the same starting blocks and success looks different to different people. It is good to realise that not all wealth is due to hard work, and not all poverty is due to laziness. Sometimes circumstances override perseverance, in the short term at least.

You may not have been brought up in a family that dealt with money well. Debt might have been the norm and rolling from one loan to the next may have been standard. It is easy for people to make judgements. Not everyone was exposed to positive money attitudes and some people are born into families that never learned how to save or even how to get a job. Understand where you are in life and harness it to grow. Keep this in mind when forming opinions about others, including yourself.

I was lucky, I grew up in a standard, middle-class household. I did not endure harrowing poverty. However, what I did know from an early age was work. From the moment I was old enough to pick fruit in the summer, I was out in the fields. I couldn't have been more than five or six when I started. That was my summer holiday. From that point onwards, I was either in school or working, or both. From that early start in life, I learned to count on myself. You must do the same.

How to Become Successful

Being successful in life does not always come down to grand gestures or significant actions. It is about doing the small things well consistently. Managing your money is the same: you don't have to take risky bets or live on the edge of life's get-rich-quick schemes, hoping for a big payoff one day. You simply have to move consistently, keep a level head when everyone is losing theirs and don't mess up just enough to get by. Do this for long enough, and you're on to a winner. Avoiding crippling life mistakes, the biggest of which is burying yourself in mountains of debt, is more potent than any tempting get-rich tip or investing advice.

Everything has a price. The price of a high income and busy career is often time away from family. The price of a good return in the stock market is white-knuckling it during times of volatility. Everything worthwhile comes with a price and that price is often hidden. You need to understand the actual cost of what it is that you want and be willing to pay that price. You have to think about not only how you are going to live through the good times, but also the bad times. Busts are as frequent as booms, but a hundred times scarier. We are on a perpetual roller coaster and it is equally important to be prepared for the good times as the bad.

What Money Really Buys

Having money can save you money. If you have money, you can buy things that don't wear out as often. Cars with a better safety record become possible. Higher quality purchases reduce the amount spent on replacements and maintenance. Better quality food can be bought, which could lead to overall better health outcomes in later life. Having money reduces the need to pay interest or fees on overdrafts and loans.

Money cannot directly buy happiness, but it can buy security, health-care and peace of mind. Mindful spending is not about frugality, hoarding or getting the lowest price. It is more about being a good steward of the limited resources that you are given. Time, health and security are some of those limited resources. Mindful spending allows you to save in some areas so that you can spend in others.

Money doesn't have to be earmarked for a particular purchase. Money saved represents a choice. It is worth having savings even when you are not sure what you want to buy with them. Sometime in the future you might want or need something. If you have savings, you just might be able to afford that thing. The feeling of knowing that you can walk straight into a shop and buy a big-ticket item for cash is a mighty good feeling indeed.

When it comes to money and return on investments, it is essential to realise that the highest dividend that money can pay is time. Making money work so hard for you that you get back time and build your autonomy over that time is the most significant wealth any person can have. The goal is full control over every moment of your life and not to be beholden to those around you. Being able to do what you want, when you want, with whomever you want for as long as you want is the key to long-lasting happiness and a fulfilling life.

No amount of fancy material things, homes or cars can ever substitute for this. The enjoyment of having fancy stuff wears thin quickly. However, having a job that you love, with flexible hours and a short commute, will never get old. Having a Rainy-Day Fund set aside for times of uncertainty will never get old. Knowing that whatever happens, there is a cushion to fall on, giving you the time and space to plan what you want with your life, will never get old.

In saying that, there is a balance that must be achieved. Knowing how to save consistently and living below your means – without extreme frugality that would hurt your quality of life – is just as important. Financial independence is an admirable goal to have; however, it is not an all or nothing choice. Every cent and euro set aside is an extra slice of freedom for you. Every bit of personal wealth built brings more of your time under your control and allows you to schedule that time according to your priorities and not someone else's.

As I've mentioned, the highest dividend money pays is time. How many times have you pined over buying something and then gotten it only to find out that it didn't make you nearly as happy as you thought it would? The happiness spike that you get from that thing lasts only so long, and then you come back to baseline. The novelty wears off and you realise that it does not bring the happiness that it promised. Having a sense of control over your life, however, brings overall joy up. The feeling of control – feeling like you can plan out your days, weeks, months and years and have the power to do so – is so freeing. This sense of autonomy over your time actually leads to higher overall happiness. Control brings contentment that is intoxicating.

Once you begin to view choices and actions through this lens, you will start to see what money can really buy. It buys time, autonomy and creativity. Money buys freedom.

Part III

MINDFUL SPENDING AND YOUR VALUE SYSTEM

7

MINDFUL SPENDING

Money is an emotional thing. We carry deep feelings towards it and about it throughout our lives. Experiences from childhood and how our parents related to it can mould our long-term relationships with money. Some can be positive; however, unfortunately, many are negative.

Have you ever:

- Felt guilty for spending money?
- Suffered buyer's remorse?
- Struggled to make purchasing decisions?
- Felt fear at the thought of managing a budget?
- Dreaded dealing with bills and other expenses?

If any of these resonate with you, then a mindful spending lifestyle could be for you. By understanding your negative spending emotions, you can start to heal them and go on to build good mindful spending habits that will stand you in good stead for the rest of your life.

WHAT IS MINDFUL SPENDING?

What if there was a way to save money without feeling like you're missing out? What if there was a way to feel right about every euro spent? If there was a way to know that when a transaction is made, it is contributing to your overall happiness and long-term financial health? With mindful spending, we are shifting our mindset from 'I see it, I want it' to 'Do I need it, and will it bring value to my life?'

The concept of mindfulness has gained popularity in recent times. Mindfulness is the practice of maintaining a non-judgemental awareness of one's thoughts, emotions and experiences in the moment. In other words, it is being focused on the present moment and nowhere else. Mindful spending is a sister to mindfulness, with the difference that it is applied to money and the value that money can bring to your life. Mindful spending is the habit of maintaining awareness of the thoughts, emotions or experiences you have in association with money and how you perceive it.

Being mindful with money is spending it consciously or intentionally. It guides you to think about how you feel and act with all expenditures. Mindful spending uses your emotions to create a sustainable, satisfying way to manage money.

Mindful spending is about finding happiness and satisfaction in every euro spent. Deriving pleasure from each transaction allows less money overall to be spent as your needs and wants are met more efficiently, with less money wasted on things that don't make a difference. This lends itself to achieving a greater sense of happiness and allows you to save and put the balance to work in building the life that you want. The payoff, in terms of increased quality of life, can be dramatic.

Mindful spending is a long-term lifestyle choice. If you have ever struggled with money, be it spending too much or indeed too little, this can help. Even if you don't have an issue with spending, adopting mindful spending will enhance your life as it will help you to make the best choices that align with who you are and the values that you have. Mindful spending is feeling good about what you're spending money on. It's about knowing what your goals and values are and spending money in a way that aligns with them.

Sometimes it can seem like saving is analogous to deprivation, like you can't save unless you're depriving yourself of something you enjoy. You're supposed to feel bad when you do spend money. Who wants to spend their life this way? I certainly don't. Following the habits in this book will eradicate any sense of deprivation or frugality and replace them with feelings of abundance and joy.

WHY IS IT SO HARD TO CURB SPENDING?

The reason is simple: we are surrounded by messages that tell us that because we are so busy, we deserve a treat, a break, a new toy to play with. We are surrounded by consumerism and a 'buy me' mentality. So often we are told (with great urgency, I might add) that our lives would not be complete without whatever it is that they are selling. The fear of missing out (FOMO) is real. Billions of euros are spent each year to make us part with our hard-earned cash and consume things we don't need. We are social creatures and want to fit in, and so we do what we are told and dutifully purchase without thinking about why we are really doing it. The result is that we burn through money with nothing tangible to show for it, other than a hole in our bank account and a heap of crumpled receipts.

Retail therapy is a trap. Pause to consider how you spend your money – how do you feel about these expenditures? Is your spending helping or hurting your future? Is shopping keeping you from facing something difficult inside you? Those complicated feelings won't go away because of a day out with the credit card. Retail therapy is a pretty expensive way to resolve nothing. It has no end and provides no cure, it is an infinity loop of wasted money and dashed hopes. Maybe life has dealt you a tough hand and you need guidance from a licensed professional. That is something that you need to decide, but I can assure you that no answers can be found at the end of till receipt.

If you need to blow off steam, find a boxing class or go for a run in the rain. Whatever you do, spending money that you don't have on things that you don't need will not do anything to make you truly happier. It will only slow your life down and make you work harder down the road to pay it back.

THE LATTE AND THE DANISH

The next time you order a double shot mocha latte and Danish, stop and think about whether you even want them. Did you smell the rich coffee aroma as you walked by the cafe and decide on impulse? Do you buy them regularly out of mindless habit, unconsciously munching while thinking of other things? Alternatively, do you lunch there regularly out of convenience? If the answer is either of the first two, not only are you consuming hundreds of empty calories, but you're also spending money on things that aren't adding to your overall happiness or health. Like lots of tasty treats, the satisfaction from the first bite or two is gone by the third or fourth. Pause to think about what you could do differently. Think about what effect you're actually looking for. If you need caffeine and sugar to wake up, consider going to bed earlier to get more sleep or exercising in the morning to get your blood pumping. Both will give you more energy without ensuring a sugar crash later, and both are better for your health and pocket. Spend less while increasing happiness.

However, if you are meeting a friend and you haven't treated yourself to a bun and coffee in a long time, things might look different. The occasion is a planned, long-awaited treat and the catch-up is enjoyed and remembered. In this case it might be an excellent use of your money. Mindful spending is ultimately about bringing thoughtfulness to how money is spent to make your life better. It's about tapping into your positive emotional forces to achieve a life you love, using the money you have.

Autopilot Is the Default Mode

Over the last couple of decades, the average savings rate in Ireland has been low. That means that people were going into debt faster than they were saving. It's so easy to put all those small purchases on a credit card. They don't seem like much, individually. But the monthly credit card statement can provide a bit of a shock when you see how quickly it all adds up. As mentioned earlier, only 40 per cent of Irish households are saving, and much of that is to pay off existing debt. So one would have to consider if anyone is really saving at all.

Let's look at the lack of saving in a real-life context for a moment. Open any cupboard or press. Tell me honestly if each item was worth what you spent on it. I especially dare you to take a long look in your wardrobe and justify every piece in there as worth every cent of the hard-earned cash you handed over for it. The hours you worked to give that dress a home in your wardrobe ... you were even kind enough to leave the tags on it as it hung there for the last 18 months.

I know that I am picking on clothes here, but I think that they illustrate the point nicely. I don't know anyone who is utterly delighted with every shirt, dress, and shoe they own. The truth is that most of us are guilty of spending money without thinking about it. Think of things that have been bought in the past and question why those purchases were made. Quite often, there was no real reason for their acquisition. That spending did not have any purpose. Racking up debt due to mindless spending is wasting money. We've developed a tolerance to spending and don't feel anything when doing it. Autopilot is the default setting now. We part with our future without a second's thought or hesitation. The autopilot needs to be switched off.

MINDFUL SPENDING IS ABOUT FINDING HAPPINESS

It doesn't matter what the advert tells you. There is no one item or experience that can make you truly happy. Yes, a gadget can provide a quick fix, but real happiness? That has to come from you, through the choices you make for yourself. Mindful spending means a lifetime free from financial struggle. With mindful spending, your relationship with money moves from being an adversarial one to one of collaboration and comradeship.

Being happy is a choice, regardless of your circumstances. I don't mean that giddy, grinning-inanely-all-the-time happy. I mean glad in your heart. Happy with yourself. Content with life, your life. Mindfully spending your time and money means slowing down to consider the impact of each expenditure on you, your life, and the lives of those around you. When mindful spending is in action, your heart and mind together lead the charge in all your spending choices. You will gradually begin spending in a way both your brain and your heart agree on.

Mindful spending will not necessarily give back more time, at least not right away. However, it will ensure that the time spent with your money is a more fulfilling, less stressful and happier experience. No one wants to spend life stressing over their balance sheets. Once your income is substantially higher than your outgoings, the mind can relax and enjoy living, safe in the knowledge that everything is under control. Mindful spending is knowing how your spending supports your goals, values and needs.

THE BENEFITS OF MINDFUL SPENDING

Mindful spending is making sure that all those hours you put in at work mean something.

1. It helps you to value your time and who you are.
2. It ensures that your house isn't filled with clutter and clothes that still have tags on them.
3. It reduces the amount of money frittered away on impulse.
4. It allows you to save more without feeling deprived.
5. It is better for the environment as we buy fewer things of better quality.
6. It reduces the likelihood you will need to draw down debt.
7. It helps to eliminate existing debt faster.
8. It gives you more control over your life.
9. It gives you the freedom to make choices for your life and not to pay back someone else.
10. It helps you to build your life on your own terms.

GOOD THINGS TAKE TIME

Mindful spending takes time, practice and patience. If you decide to take control of your financial future, these habits will be the key to unlocking money you already have. Transitioning from a conventional, consumption-driven mindset to a mindful spending mindset can take time. Some find it a little challenging to change the habit of a lifetime. If changing habits were that easy, we would all be super-rich, super-fit and have six-pack abs. Changing habits is hard, and it needs consistent practice. That said, changing a habit, no matter how ingrained, is very possible, and its positive effects will permeate all areas of your life.

When consistently implemented, mindful spending dives deep into your heart. You discover your life passions and most definite values, and spending becomes a means of supporting your unique life desires. Mindful spending is a simple but effective lifestyle-based money management technique that can empower you to live your best life. Applying mindful spending will shape your lifestyle to be uniquely yours. Soon the Joneses will be jealous of you.

8

VALUES

Values are part of who we are. They highlight what we stand for and represent our unique, individual essence. Values guide our behaviour, providing us with a personal code of conduct. When our spending decisions and core values harmonise, we experience fulfilment. When they do not, things don't feel right, and we are likely to escape into unhelpful old habits or abstain from making the decisions needed to push us forward.

Every spending decision made actively engages the heart, from the snack bar at the checkout to your car insurance renewal. Whether you're aware of it or not, the heart has its say. Science has proven we make decisions with emotions, not logic. We may think that our capable and educated minds make these decisions, but this is not the case. The truth is spending is first and foremost a heart-driven act.

Understanding that the heart is the real driver here makes it clear there is no getting around it. Knowing the power of the heart is why it is essential to discover what your core values are. Align them to harness the power of the habits of mindful spending. If your spending aligns with your values, then your heart will do the rest. Decisions that lead to a fulfilling life, decisions that you love, and not ones that you think that you should love, will happen naturally.

'Values are like fingerprints. Nobody's are the same but you leave 'em all over everything that you do.'

Elvis Presley

Knowing your core values is essential to living your most authentic and purposeful life. If your spending habits are a result of unhealthy motivations, such as trying to fill an emotional need or keep up with the neighbours, you will never address root problems or be truly happy in life.

What Is a Value System?

Our values form our value system. Value systems are prescriptive beliefs; they affect our moral and ethical behaviour. They are our code of conduct and are the culmination of all our core values combined.

Your value system does not have to include esoteric life goals like curing world hunger or ending all conflicts. As courageous and lofty as these ideals are, they are most probably beyond the capabilities of any one individual. However, an individual's value system can feed into the greater good, which builds towards that goal – for example, if a value is giving back, or wanting to make the world a better place. In that case, donating a portion of one's income to a particular charity might do the trick. Charities use the money they receive to make their core issue better; they pool donations and put plans in place on a bigger scale than most people could on their own. Even though you are not on the front line, you are helping people with the right skills to be there, which has a more significant impact in the long term. If everyone did this, cumulatively the effect could be immeasurable. If you choose to spend your income this way, and therefore spend less on a TV package or keep your current TV for an extra few years, for example, you can balance out this cost and it will make you happier – if that is what you value.

Another value might be the quality of food. Specifically, animal welfare, supply chains, the origins of food, or ethical, health and environmental issues may be of paramount importance to you. As a result of this value, choosing to spend more on purchasing sustainable, locally sourced or organic food might be a priority. You might feel happier and more fulfilled when you buy food in this way. To balance out the additional cost, you may decide not to upgrade to the latest phone and to move to a cheaper package. In this case, knowing you are living in alignment with who you are through food is more fulfilling than owning the latest device. Conversely, for a person who values technology, having the most up-to-date phone is vital, and paring back their wardrobe to have it is not a sacrifice.

A person may love their hair and take great pride in keeping it healthy and styled. It is a value for them. As a result, spending money on a good hair conditioner and treatment is something that makes them happier. Spending less on perfumes to free up cash for hair care isn't a big deal because healthy hair is more important than having fifteen bottles of perfume.

Another person may value financial security and getting out of debt. Paying down debt aggressively and creating savings bring a greater sense of joy and control in life. Not eating out so much or buying the latest trends pales in comparison to the feeling of satisfaction gained from knowing that they have a Rainy-Day Fund.

A parent might decide that they want to spend more time at home with the children. To do so may mean stepping back from their career for a few years. This can cause a loss of income, but once they curb their outgoings, staying at home becomes manageable. Everyone is happier overall.

Values can be anything; the only criterion for a value is how it makes you feel when you are doing it, working towards it or thinking about it. It brings something to your life that nothing else can deliver. It warms you from the inside and fits with who you are as a person, not what you think you should be or what is socially preferred.

PART IV

THE INCEPTION OF A MINDFUL SPENDING JOURNEY

9

A CAUTIONARY TALE ABOUT HOMEOWNERSHIP

When I look back on my first experience as a homeowner, I cringe. I want to hug and slap myself at the same time. A poor decision made one morning by a naive girl put in motion a series of events that crippled us financially and emotionally for almost a decade. When I play it back in my mind it unfolds like something out of a comedy sketch. The audience can see what is happening, but the main character is oblivious to the impending disaster. At the risk of losing all credibility here, let me entertain you with a little story of how I survived my first home.

In late 2005, before the big recession – the one that we never saw coming – money was everywhere, and it just kept on coming. Mortgage rates were low, saving interest was high, and credit cards offered limitless funds. Money was spent like it was going out of fashion, things were good and we didn't know what to do with ourselves.

I was 25, the financial boom was my normal. I was single, had only myself to think about and a paycheck to fritter away. My goodness, I did. I frittered away with the best of them. I didn't know any other world. I had no concept of saving, investing or building for the future. Pensions were for grown-ups, and whatever I was, I wasn't that yet, not by a long shot. My greatest achievement was making it into work in the morning and having enough in my account for the weekend's socialising.

At the time, TV and the media in general were awash with property shows, shows about getting on the property ladder and documentaries encouraging my age group to fly the nest and get their own first home. It was everywhere. There was tangible pressure across the nation to get my peers to become independent and give the baby boomers some much-needed space. The buzz word was 'starter home', and the push was on to have one of your own. I was not immune to the peer pressure. After all, I was 25, in Ireland, and the best way to prove how grown-up you were was to saddle yourself with severe debt and carry that millstone with ignorant pride.

A week or so into 2006, I decided that I was going to buy a house. No planning, no thinking and no idea how. I drove to the local town and walked into the first estate agent that I saw. He showed me some plans for houses that weren't built yet. That was all he had left; things were selling fast. Two greenfield sites, a pair of filthy heels and a lot of imagination later, I handed over my credit card and hey presto, I had put down a holding deposit on my non-existent house with my non-existent savings.

I had just impulse-bought a house, an overpriced house based on the plans for it. Now, I had to figure out how to pay for it. Being the naive creature that I was, I was not going to let a detail like that stop me. I waltzed into my local bank with the estate agent's brochure in hand, decorated with the artist's impression of my non-existent house. I explained that I wanted to buy it, and 40 minutes and several signatures later I skipped out the door with approval for a 90 per cent mortgage of over seven times my income. Income from a job that I had started only 3 weeks earlier, for a house that I, in reality, had no use for.

Next, I needed to somehow find the 10 per cent deposit. One quick credit union loan later, the deposit was in my account. It didn't take much convincing of anyone. Money was handed out so easily back then. In the space of a day, I had gone from being a footloose, broke twenty-something to a super-broke indebted homeowner of a theoretical house.

Six months later, I moved into the newly built house in the middle of a half-built estate. It had no flooring, no fireplace, nothing, only a basic kitchen frame and ceramic toilets and a sink. I spent the next year living entirely off my credit card just to get basic comforts in the house. It was almost a year before I could afford a kitchen table. Nevertheless – smart me – I was on my way in life, a homeowner with a budding career. I was living the dream.

Around the time I got the sofa and TV, murmurings of a recession began to surface. I had no idea what that meant and continued my spending, unwittingly yet happily being owned by my house. A house that I decorated with the best things I couldn't afford. I bought expensive wood for the floors, branded white ware and even a marble fireplace. Around this time, I met my husband and he moved in. This would be where we would raise our family.

The recession stormed in, and soon the house was only worth half of what it had been bought for. Building around us came to a standstill, leaving us stuck in a development that got the well-deserved label of 'ghost estate'; a half-built development with all the associated problems. What could have been a beautiful area with a great sense of community went downhill fast. My husband's employer went to the wall, I was barely hanging on to my job, and I found out I was pregnant with my second child. We had no choice but to hang on for the ride.

Eventually, my husband did land a new job. however, it was several counties away. We moved out of the mortgaged house and rented a place near his new role. The financial burden of paying rent, rearing two children and maintaining a mortgage for an empty home was hard. The financial burden rested heavily on us both. I had two beautiful babies who needed me at my best, but I can tell you now, I was not at my best. To bring in additional income, we decided to rent the house.

10

HOW NOT TO RENT OUT A HOUSE

After meeting several potential renters, we settled on a family: a husband, wife and three boys. I rang their references, they were all glowing. They moved in straight away, and things went smoothly for the first few months. They seemed happy with the house. Anything that needed fixing or replacing was attended to straight away. I thought that if I was a kind landlord, then they would be good tenants. Unfortunately, these things don't always pan out.

All was well for about six months, and then things began to change. Rent became sporadic. I would be told that money was tight, or that work was in short supply. The recession was hard on everyone, and they sounded so sincere. I was consistently assured that this was temporary, that they would catch up. I fell for the excuses, but as time passed, the rent stopped entirely.

Not long after, I got a call from a neighbour, wondering what I was going to do with the house. Was I putting it on the market or getting new renters? As far as I was aware, the tenants were still there, they were just going through a tough time – we all were. It was a recession; life was hard for everyone. I tried to contact them, with no luck. Left with no choice but to check things out for myself, I bundled the children into the car and made the journey. From the outside the house looked dishevelled. The curtains were drawn and I could see no sign of life. Entering without permission was not a possibility, so I called down to the local Garda station and explained my case. A kind Garda accompanied me to the house. We unlocked the front door and I nearly cried at what I saw.

The house had been cleared out; the few remaining items were beyond repair. The furniture, appliances, beds – everything was gone. I subsequently found out they had been sold on an online auction site. There was rubbish piled in the garden and debt collectors' bills stacked in the front hallway, alongside unpaid utility bills. Rats had infested the garage, the toilets were all blocked, and fittings had been pulled off the walls. In short, the house had been gutted, and its occupants disappeared. I felt for the Garda, and she felt for me. There was nothing she could say or do. I had no idea where they had gone and no clue what to do next. So I locked the door, bundled my kids back into our beat-up old car and made the two-hour trip back to our rented home.

The next couple of months tested us. In Ireland, a landlord received little support at the time. I didn't have a forwarding address. I had no recourse for the rent or the stolen items. It would have taken more money than we had to make it rentable again. We were deep in negative equity for a house that had been looted of most of its contents. The only option was to put it on the market and get what we could for it. It sold a short time later, for half what it was bought for, and we absorbed the loss and carried the debt with us.

I fully understand that our situation was exceptional and that the majority of renters are good, hard-working people. I also understand that there are below-par landlords, who do not act as they should. However, there is also a grey area, where careless tenants and inexperienced landlords meet, and this is not a place I recommended anyone find themselves in.

It was a time that I never want to live through again. That said, I don't feel hard done by because of this experience anymore. I did for some time – it devastated our finances, and my mental health took a beating. A mortgage is a big deal and I had completely underestimated its gravity. It became a millstone around my neck and, subsequently, my husband's neck. It demanded all our financial resources, energy and time for years.

There is little point in crying into my coffee and saying that no one warned me against it because no one told me to do it, either. I just went along with the crowd, without considering where it was going. I got into my car and drove to the estate agent, I signed on the dotted line for that mortgage. That was me and me alone. What possessed me to buy a house in the first place I will never fully understand. It was my fault for not thinking it through. There is no accounting for the stupidity of not thinking for myself.

It was this event that made me promise that I would never put my family in such a vulnerable position again. The stress of being so deep in debt caused us to be at the mercy of the jobs market. It also made us very sensitive to changes in the economy. These were things that we could never control.

However, there were other things that I could manage. I tasked myself with reading and learning as much as I could about money and personal finance. Concurrently, we threw ourselves into work, willing participants in the great rat race revolving around crèches and commuting. It was hard going, but we had a big hole in our finances to fill. Little by little, the plan began to show results. Slowly, we built up savings and paid off debts. Things started to look up; we were on a steady path to financial security. That was until I handed in my notice and walked away from a 16-year career.

11

THE INCEPTION OF THE NO-SPEND YEAR

I gripped the steering wheel, bawling my eyes out in the car park, mourning something I had voluntarily given up. How did I get to this point? How did I end up walking away from a 16-year career? One that was key to building up the financial security that I so badly craved. What had pushed me to do this? I will tell you what drove me: my kids pushed me, and here's how. It was my son's junior infants year; I took a day off, deciding to surprise him by collecting him from school. I lined up with the other parents in the yard, watching them chatter comfortably with one another, catching up on the local news. I did not know any of them or manage to associate them with a child I knew, because in reality I knew practically none. I waited on my own for the bell to ring and mark the day's end. The children came out one by one, released by the teacher as she spotted each parent and sent the corresponding child out to them. I waited and waited, but there was no sign of my son.

As the yard cleared, I was the only parent left. The others had moved away, busy with their daily errands. I approached the teacher to inquire about my son. I hadn't met her before as my husband did the drop-offs and our childminder collected the children. She kindly asked who I was, as she did not recognise me, and understandably could not release my son to me. My boy heard my voice and came bounding out and into my arms. I explained who I was, and the misunderstanding was quickly cleared up. We bundled ourselves into the car and headed to the local park.

We had an hour to ourselves before it was time to collect his older sister. I couldn't fault the teacher, the school, or the policy. It was a lovely comfort to see first-hand how seriously they took their child protection policy. However, what it did do was reflect poorly on my life and how little I was around. It hurt to have my reality put in front of me like that. It hurt badly. I was his mother and I wasn't there.

My son chattered and bounced around telling me about his day; he was excited to see me so early. The usual routine didn't have me home until dinner or sometime after. My mind was stuck at that moment, that awful moment, when I almost didn't get to collect him. His teacher had not known who I was. She knew my husband, she knew my childminder, but I was an absolute stranger to her. This new awareness only stung more as I soaked up my son's excitement. He revelled in spending this stolen time with me. Guilt weighed heavily on me. I suggested we play on the swings.

The second blow came when I had a particularly busy run at work that coincided with a course I was doing. The demands on my time intensified and I found that I was spending more and more time away from home. I was tired, but I knew that I had to persist with this workload. After all, I was a professional and a responsible adult. It had to be done. I lost myself in this world of important tasks until one Sunday morning my daughter asked me where I was going that day.

I laughed and said, 'Why nowhere, dear, it's Sunday, I have a house to clean'. Her eyes lit up, and she clapped her hands, 'Oh, Mom! How amazing, I get to see you today!' I was about to reply, 'But honey you get to see me every day'. But before the words left my lips, I caught them, and realised that would have been a lie. I had not seen my kids awake for an entire week. I snuck into their rooms and kissed their sweaty foreheads before I left each morning, repeating the process in the evening. I had seen them, but they had not seen me. What struck me about her reaction was that she was genuinely content with piecemeal access to her mom, even if I was also busy mopping floors and catching up on washing. Another episode that reflected poorly on the meted-out parent time that my children had become accustomed too.

Workwise, my husband's job and mine were city-based, so we chose the home that we thought was best for the kids, within the limitations of what we could afford, which meant that we lived in the commuter belt. It also implied that we were committed to long commutes each day.

When we bought, Ireland was recovering from the recession and traffic had seemed reasonable enough. As time went by and the country inched closer to full employment, the main arteries into Dublin grew increasingly clogged; idling in traffic had become a national pastime. The time to get up in the morning sneakily became earlier and earlier, while the evening arrival home became later and later. Both of us were spending longer away from the home and kids we loved so much.

The constant breakneck speed of our lives was taking its toll on all of us, children included, despite maintaining as good a routine as possible each day. My husband would drop the kids off at school. Our childminder would collect them and care for them until I got home. Unfortunately, this often ended up being at the same time or later than my husband's return. Our family time was continually squeezed. Our children were consistently farmed out so they could fit into our busy professional lives. We seemed to be ships passing in the night, always off to do something and never stopping to catch our breaths. Life was passing us by, and we hadn't even looked up to notice.

I was stuck, torn between two worlds. I was missing watching my kids grow up, but it would be ridiculous to walk away from my career after all those years. I was responsible for half the household income. It would be entirely unfair to push the whole financial burden onto my husband's shoulders, especially in this country, with its high cost of living. But was this the price I wanted to pay for financial security and a particular lifestyle? Did I enjoy my career that much?

The final push came one morning at 5.30 a.m. while I was sitting in heavy traffic. I hadn't moved in almost twenty minutes and knew from experience that this meant yet another broken-down car ahead. This fender bender would add an extra hour my journey. I let out a sigh and stared into the pouring rain ahead. The only sounds were the rhythm of the wipers and the low hum of combustion engines in the morning darkness; the modern dawn chorus. I turned on a podcast, to help pass the time. I cannot remember the name of the guest, but I will find him someday and shake his hand. He spoke at length about priorities and values, but one statement stood out above all others.

'A parent spends 95 per cent of their time with their children when they are children.'

In the morning twilight, I could feel the mirror being held up once more. I think this time the mirror cracked entirely.

12

THE MOST SIGNIFICANT DECISION OF MY LIFE

Time spent cleaning is my thinking time. I have found over the years that if I want to mull over a problem, I do it best with a rag and spray bottle in hand. It was during one of these cleans that I picked up a vase to dust. I stopped for the first time in forever to look at it. I mean really look at it. This vase had been carefully packed and unpacked through various house moves. It was washed, dusted and polished, it was angled, adjusted and filled with flowers on occasion. I had invested a relatively large amount of time and money into this simple vase. Now looking at it properly I realised that I didn't even like it that much. I don't think that I ever had. So why had I poured so much energy into it?

The answer was disappointingly easy. I bought it as an accent piece because a magazine told me that my sitting room wouldn't be complete without it. This was an aha moment for me. I began to look at my home differently, in a way that I never had before. Why did I have many of the things that I had? When I thought about it, I honestly had no idea why most of it was there or what I was doing with it. Boxes filled with stuff, with no clue what the items were. Very little of it had a proper use or made me recall a fond memory. These unnecessary things added up to a princely sum. The money we had worked hard for and gave up of chunks of our adult life for – and for what? We didn't need any of this. I was spending large chunks of my precious time cleaning, mending and minding these irrelevant things. Time that could have been spent with my children.

I didn't feel any wittier, wealthier or more interesting for having these things. I didn't feel much at all except that they represented an extra responsibility in an already busy life. I knew that most of these things were there because I thought that I should have them. They were things that clever people had, 'must-haves' for those with busy lives. They showed how important and educated I was, or, let's be honest and more precise here, who I thought I was supposed to be. I didn't need these things to make me happy. What I wanted was more time to enjoy my life and my family. Yet here I was in a perpetual cycle of more and more stuff. It was suffocating. I had thought that having a home filled with tasteful articles would make me more satisfied with life, but in the light of my squeezed time and family discontent, it all seemed excessive and, frankly, ridiculous. These were other people's ideas of tasteful articles and full lives, not mine.

When had I stopped thinking for myself? I had enough stuff; I had my fill of things and clutter. What I needed now was time, and the freedom to spend that time with my kids. What I also needed was all the money back that I had wasted over the years on unnecessary, useless things. Gadgets, clothes with tags on, barely opened makeup and other frivolous spends lurked in every drawer of my home, grim reminders of my wasteful spending habits. Was this what I was trading my life for? These items seemed so shallow now and only convinced me that I was an easy target for the advertising industry.

It felt like my idea of who I was, and who I was supposed to be, or what I was supposed to want or need, was not of my creation. I was beginning to question the very notion of who I was and what I needed. When I was frank with myself, I did not know who I was any more. Years before, before marriage, before kids, I knew who I was. Not now, though, now I was in new territory, and life had not slowed down to let me catch my breath. It appeared to have only increased in velocity and dissuaded me from getting my bearings. When had I stopped being me and started being someone that I thought I was supposed to be?

Aware of the shortcomings in my life, it was on me to change it into something that worked. Being confronted with my wasteful spending, compounded by the expense of childcare and the costs incurred by me just going to work, I finally began to see an alternative path forming. It scared the heck out of me. It would mean me letting go of a massive part of who I was and what I loved. It would mean that I would have to deal with all sorts of opinions and criticisms by going against the grain. What it would also mean was that I just might be able to walk that thin tightrope of a life of no regrets.

With that tiny seed of a desire to change beginning to sprout, I started to believe that an alternative life could be possible. This plan would mean that we would lose my income entirely. This would be a hard blow to our finances. However, and more importantly, it would give me the chance to spend crucial time with my growing children. Done correctly, it would help to tilt the needle in our favour. We could cut our outgoings significantly by slashing our spending and embracing minimalism. I couldn't fool myself into thinking that I could replace my entire income by cutting back. However, maybe, just maybe, if I worked it right, I could spend the small window of their childhood with them, without decimating our finances.

It was time to bring my plan to my husband, but I found myself procrastinating. I tried to begin the conversation several times but lost my nerve each time. I was desperately nervous; I would be asking for something so big from him and felt massively guilty doing so. He already worked so hard and had taken up the slack when I was juggling work and a Master's. Here I was thanking him by overturning the carefully balanced apple cart that was our life.

When I finally summoned the courage to tell him what I wanted, all I remember was the look of relief on his face. He felt the pressure of perpetually being late into work due to school runs, and absorbing the workload when I was not at home. He missed me, but he knew how much my career meant to me. He never complained; he just kept going because he loved me and wanted me to be happy. I hadn't considered the pressure that both of us working and juggling our lives had put on him, too. I don't think that I've ever loved him any more than I did at that moment.

With my husband on board, I steeled myself, poised to take control of our lives and make a new life work for us. I now had a way that not only allowed us to pursue the same goal, but that would make for a far more intriguing journey. So with a deep breath, and excited pain in my chest, I sat down and penned the letter. It was one of the most daring moments of my life. Once I did this, there was no turning back. I was changing the trajectory of not only my own life but that of my kids and husband forever. That letter was my letter of resignation and the journey was the No-Spend Year.

PART V

THE HABITS OF MINDFUL SPENDING

13

HABIT 1: PAY YOURSELF FIRST

Every morning, you turn off the alarm while yearning to roll back over for some more blissful sleep. You can't, you have a job to do. A job that you work hard for, one that, at the end of the week or month, pays a nice sum into your account. This is your thanks for a job well done. You have worked hard for this money; you have earned it. It is the fruit of your labour. Hooray for you. You are rich! Temporarily, at least.

This may be the only money you have to fund every aspect of your life. It may be the sole resource to pay bills, go on holidays, fix the car, save for the future, eat. Unless you have a rich relative tucked away somewhere, or the lottery gods shine on you, this is it. The content of that account is the total you have to build your life. So why is it that so much is frittered away without thinking? Mindlessly tapping the card again, and again, until there is nothing left but an empty account, and no idea where most of it went. What is there to show for all those early mornings and time away from your loved ones? Why does it seem that there is so much month left at the end of the money? Is it worth it?

Earning a paycheck is important. However, what you do with the money is even more important. Building the future of your dreams is less about your level of income and more about what you do with that income. Even if your salary isn't through the roof, there are ways to make it last longer and build something great. It is on you to make it work as hard for you as you had to work to get it. I will show you the tool, all you need to do is pick that tool up.

WHAT IS PAY YOURSELF FIRST?

Pay Yourself First is a powerful mindful money habit. It is the first step in a system that allows you to build your net worth and transform pipe dreams into reality. Without it, you are little more than a middle person in the great cash flow of life.

If you have been inconsistent or less than successful at putting money aside for yourself in the past, this habit is an easy way to get on track. By making Pay Yourself First a priority, you allow yourself to form new habits, ones that really provide results. To understand this concept is to understand your real value and the value that you bring to your work, your life and the people in it. This habit has a massive effect on not only net worth but also self-worth.

In simple terms, Pay Yourself First is the practice of putting money aside for yourself before all else. A set amount of money is put aside each pay period before bills, before groceries, before any other payment is made. Pay Yourself First needs to be the first 'bill' every month. It does not matter how small this amount is in the beginning, it only matters that you always do it, without exception. It has to be the first outgoing before life gets in the way.

Once Pay Yourself First money is set aside, it is out of sight and not sitting in your bank account, tempting you. This is the money used for saving, building deposits, overpaying on a mortgage, investing and pensions. This money is the only money that you have genuinely earned and makes up the building blocks you need to live a secure life. Any other cash spent only serves to pay for a lifestyle and little else. The bottom line is that if you do not prioritise this mindful habit, then another week or month has slipped by where you have worked for nothing except to pay other people. Why be a middleman in your own life?

If you think that putting money aside before other bills is impossible, think again. How many times have you spent years paying off a loan, diligently paying the premium each month? You came up with that money even when times were hard. Once the loan was repaid, you thought you had lots of money to save and build with, but before you knew it, you were trying to make ends meet again. There is nothing to spare and you wonder how you were ever able to make that repayment in the first place. The reason you could pay the loan was that you prioritised that specific bill. You gave that money a job to do. You knew there would be negative repercussions if you didn't. That bill was essential for you to repay. Once the loan cleared, that money didn't have a job, and so dissipated into the ether of life. Pay Yourself First needs to have the same level of priority as those types of commitment.

Putting money aside for you first will not only lessen the chance of you needing future loans, it puts you back in the driver's seat of life.

THE TRADITIONAL SPENDING MINDSET LETS US DOWN

Traditionally, many of us tend to pay everyone else first. When it comes to saving, it's is often left until the end of the pay period in the hope that there will be something left to save. In truth, this is rarely the case.

The traditional way tends to flow like this; payday comes round, each bill takes its pound of flesh, loans, debts and credit card balances command their portion. Other expenses that arise during the month – food, a wedding, furnishings, home maintenance, eating out, clothes, shiny new gadgets, take-aways, cosmetics, memberships, subscriptions and socialising all absorb their portion, too. These combine to soak up much of the remaining balance, leaving little if anything for saving.

Sometimes things can get even worse. Sometimes there is not enough money left to cover those unnecessary outgoings, let alone save. This is when the credit card takes a bashing, the overdraft is eaten into, or loans are taken out. Each transaction pushes you further and further away from your money and deeper and deeper into debt.

Putting expenses on the credit card because there is not enough money available to pay for these impulse buys is doubly detrimental. Not only do these expenses become next month's problem, but they also eat into your already overstretched income. The trouble is not only the amount spent but the interest accrued. This makes the impulsive splurge, the one you've already forgotten about, even more expensive. This impulse buy has become a debt. A debt that hangs on your neck is like a millstone growing more massive and more costly with time. The next pay period is harder but, even worse, saving becomes an even tougher challenge. There isn't a hope of getting out of this cycle if habits don't change.

We all want to build a lovely life, who wouldn't? We all want money to draw on when things get tough or to buy that house or to invest. However, choosing the traditional path by not prioritising saving is a sure way of making life hard for yourself. Leaving saving to be the last bill of the month means that everyone else is paid first and you get paid last, if you get paid at all. If you are not prioritising your future, then how do you expect to build the life you want? The traditional way of saving makes putting money away harder and often becomes an impossible task. Scrambling for the dregs that are left over after the month is done wringing you out is a disheartening cycle to be in. You need to break out.

LEAN INTO YOUR VALUE SYSTEM

By Paying Yourself First, you are choosing to value yourself and the work you do. The money that is set aside here is the actual amount that you earned. Everything else is just passing through, funding other people's lives, not yours. Once it is spent it is not your money anymore. It never was. The only money that is yours to keep and build with is the Pay Yourself First money.

Paying yourself first is made easier if you know your value system and lean into it. Knowing what you really want out of life will make prioritising your goals easier. It will make giving your money a job easier. Living according to your values will make you happy, and who doesn't like to put money towards things that make them truly happy? The world is a busy place, if you don't prioritise Pay Yourself First, no one else will.

DO YOU LIKE YOUR JOB THAT MUCH?

This habit makes all that time devoted to your job worthwhile. You may like your job, you may even love your job, but would you do it if there was no money involved? Or if you had to make do with small, varying amounts, or sometimes nothing at all? My guess is that you would be out of there faster than anything.

Work is trading time for money. Your precious time, experience, training, dedication and skillset are of enormous value, no matter what your job is. The culmination of who you are and what you bring to the table is essential to keep the economy going and growing. Companies and business need you and the unique mix that you bring. That is why they are more than happy to pay you for the time you give. You apply your skills for their benefit and in return for handing over this time, time that you can never get back, a salary is provided as compensation. The economic wheel turns.

Business values you and your skillset enough to part with its hard-earned cash to pay you. A business pays you first because you are an asset to them. You help that business to perform a vital function so they can grow their bottom line. Why can't you value yourself in the same way? You are the CEO of your own life, start acting like it.

Money will not put itself into savings; it does not have a mind of its own. Left to its own devices, money will disappear into other people's pockets – other people who will give it a job and put it to work. When every euro you earn is given clear direction, you will find it to be obedient and loyal.

THE BENEFITS OF PAY YOURSELF FIRST

1. It Is Your Wealth Builder

Pay Yourself First money is the point of origin of all savings, pension and investing resources. This money is beholden to no one else, only you. This is your real wealth.

2. Empowering

By doing this one act, you are justifying all those years of education, training and experience. You are ensuring a return on all those early mornings, late nights and stressful projects. You are empowering yourself to take pride in your earning ability and ensuring not only your own financial security but that of those you love.

Knowing that you are actively taking control of your money and setting security aside consciously and consistently each month is an empowering place to be.

3. It Develops Good Money Habits

The act of prioritising you in your income puts you back in the driver's seat with your money and, quite honestly, your life. Many spend money in the following order: bills, discretionary, then savings. Although the savings part rarely seems to happen as often as it should. Once the order is changed and savings are put first, all three magically become workable. The sequence then becomes: Pay Yourself First for a month's good work, you've earned it. Next, the bills and whatever is left over can be spent as desired, guilt-free.

4. You're Prepared for Whatever Life Throws at You

By paying yourself first, you are building up an ever-growing cash buffer. Each successive month makes you more and more resilient. Whatever surprises occur in life, you are ready for them. It puts you in a position to take advantage of opportunities and to weather economic storms.

HOW TO PAY YOURSELF FIRST

The smart way to Pay Yourself First is to make the process as easy and as simple as possible. Make it automatic and make it invisible.

If possible, arrange to have money taken from your salary before you receive it. Many employers can do this in the form of a pension. A pension is an excellent way to pay yourself: it's a long-term savings plan specifically for the years when you may not be able to work or may not want to work. If your employer has a pension plan, enrol as soon as possible, especially if the company matches your contributions. It is one of the only times in life where you will get free money. It is free money from your employer and free money from the government. Max it out every year if possible.

Set up direct debits for savings, college, deposits, mortgage overpayments and any other area that needs attention. Set up automatic transfers, either directly from your salary or as regular standing orders as soon as your salary hits. Treat these transfers like you'd treat any other essential bill. Make these the first and most important bills of the month. Do this first, and you'll never notice that it's missing.

How Much Should I Pay Myself?

The short answer is as much as humanly possible. If money is tight, don't be afraid to start small. (By the way, money is always tight, that will never change until you change.) Start with 1 per cent of your income, just one cent from every euro that you work hard to take home. If that still seems like a challenge then try €20 or €50 for your first couple of months. It doesn't matter how small the number is to start with, as long as you start.

Each amount put aside proves to you that it can be done. Once you have succeeded in this task, pat yourself on the back and see if you can funnel 3 per cent, 5 per cent or 10 per cent towards your savings.

Keep doing this until you have found your optimum level of saving. For some of us it will be 10 per cent, for others it will be 50 per cent or more. There is no hard rule on this, and there is no upper limit to the level of savings that you can have. We are all starting from different places. There is nothing wrong with that. Every child must learn to grasp the Lego before they can become a master builder. We cheer our children on knowing that they can do it, so do the same for yourself. Embrace the Pay Yourself First habit and be your own cheerleader.

Avoid Lifestyle Inflation and Power Up Instead

Windfalls, pay rises and bonuses should not be taken for granted. They are sporadic and never guaranteed. These are security-building gifts. You may have been lucky for the last few years and gotten a consistent bonus, but that can change at any time. These windfalls are your magic money, money that you can to use to supercharge your savings, pension, or maybe rapid debt paydown. This money is not for wasting on some material goods that you'll end up donating in a few years. Make it count.

Other magic money is the money that is freed up after a debt has been paid off. Let's say a car loan costing €200 per month comes to an end. Congratulations, you have freed yourself from that millstone, and you are now the proud owner of said vehicle. In reality, you are more than that. You are also the master of a new €200 to build with. Do not let this money go into the general coffers. You did not have this money to spend when the loan was being paid down and you got along fine. You do not need it now. This is substantial building money; it needs to be respected as such. Simply keep your current outgoings as they are and increase your savings by that amount. Keep doing this until you are maxing out your pension, debt has been eradicated, and you have a healthy savings fund to weather any storm.

Once these critical things are safely dealt with, you can loosen the purse strings again. This might mean that your standard of living stays the same for a few years, but it will also mean that you are creating healthy, mindful spending habits and are setting yourself up for future success. A success that will help protect you and your loved ones for whatever life might throw at you. No one can control the economy, but we can control how well we weather it.

SUMMARY

Every cent you save has value. Each euro saved is proof of how valuable your time is and shows respect for your life energy. Your income deserves to be respected just as you do. It is the tangible result of your efforts.

Starting a Pay Yourself First habit for the first time can be challenging. Demands on our money are high. Money may not seem to stretch far enough to allow for savings. However, it is in that thought process that the problem lies. The traditional method disempowers savings by putting them last. Pay Yourself First empowers savings. Flip the priorities to let the magic happen.

By changing how saving is prioritised, you can see what a beautiful and powerful habit it is. By giving money to yourself first you are justifying going to work. If the fruits of your efforts only go to other people, then why are you getting up in the morning? Why do you bother with a gruelling career path? Understanding the why here makes Pay Yourself First not only a no-brainer but an urgent, life-saving need. The thing about prioritising savings is that by doing so, you are not only securing your financial future, you are giving yourself the best self-care package ever. You are honouring the time and energy that you give up every day in return for this hard-earned money. You are protecting your loved ones from being blindsided in life now and in the future.

We all know that we should save money, that pensions are necessary, that we should pay down debt. However, this takes thought and effort. There will always be demands on our resources. The urgent bills, loans, surprise expenses, big sales or family events seem to shout the loudest. Paltry old savings are just meekly hanging around in the background. No one will prioritise your savings unless you do.

No matter what age you are or how modest your income, make Pay Yourself First a priority. Start small and build on that. You will never regret the day you started. You will only wish you started earlier.

14

HABIT 2: THE RAINY-DAY FUND

A Rainy-Day Fund is a savings account that money is only drawn from under a predetermined set of circumstances. A Rainy-Day Fund is for when you know that medium-term expenses are coming, but don't know what form they will take or when they will come knocking. It is your money pot for when things inevitably go wrong. When life throws you a curve ball, the last thing you want to be worrying about is money.

WHY NOT JUST CALL IT AN EMERGENCY FUND?

For as long as I've known about them, Rainy-Day Funds have had all sorts of names, like sinking fund, cushion fund, reserve fund, stockpile, backup money, stash, cache and, my pet peeve, emergency fund. There are times when I will use the latter phrase, but in the main, I try to avoid it.

There are two reasons for why I try to avoid the term emergency fund. Firstly, it implies that the world would want to be pretty close to a zombie apocalypse before it can be considered a viable option to tap into. Zombie apocalypses don't happen too often, and even if they did, the amount in your account would be the last thing on your mind, running for your life would take priority. As a result, many of us don't feel the urgency to have a reserve of money just lying around. There are so many immediate demands on our cash that the necessity is simply not there. This causes many emergency funds to be poorly stocked or, worse, put on the long finger, never to be started.

Secondly, if a genuine emergency does happen in life, something like a fire, car crash or health issue, insurance policies come into play. It's what they are designed for. It is the reason that we buy them, the rationale for their existence. They are there to protect us when major catastrophes occur. In a traditional emergency, the insurance policy is the go-to source of money to set things right.

If you do not have basic life, health, car and home insurance policies, I urge you to think strongly about putting them in place. If a real life-changing emergency happens, it is likely to happen suddenly and severely. This sort of event blindsides you when you least expect it. The last thing on your mind in those situations should be money.

WHY DO I NEED A RAINY-DAY FUND?

If all the significant catastrophes in life are covered by insurance, then what is the purpose of a Rainy-Day Fund? A Rainy-Day Fund is money that is set aside for the bad weather in life. Rain is always on its way; it is Ireland, after all. When it comes to our personal life, something is inevitably going to break or go wrong. We don't know if it will last a week, a month or a year, but we do know that something will need fixing and it will always find the most inconvenient time to require mending. The car will need more work than you thought, the washing machine will fill the kitchen with water, the heating will pack it in on the coldest day of the year, or there will be redundancies on the horizon.

A Rainy-Day Fund is also where the excesses of insurance policies are saved. Depending on the type of policy that you have, an excess may be stipulated. Knowing what your excess is for your policy is as important as knowing what exactly you are covered for.

No one can predict the future or what that future will bring. What we do know is that some things will happen, it's just a matter of when and where. That's life. These events, for the most part, are out of our control. However, what is within our control is to be ready for them, or not.

THE BENEFITS OF A RAINY-DAY FUND

Having a Rainy-Day Fund will help to get through the surprise events. It is there to protect you until the incident has been overcome. It is your protective raingear; the shelter to care for you while you deal with the downpour. Here are some of the critical benefits of having one.

1. Let's You Get on With Your Life

Having money put aside for life's surprises will make dealing with that surprise much more straightforward. There is no avoiding the hassle of calling the repair guy or researching a new appliance. However, those are easy to do when you don't have to cope with the stress of figuring out how it will be paid for. The Rainy-Day Fund has that part covered. All you need to focus on is getting life back on track and moving forward. Once the issue has been dealt you can carry on with life and there is no extra money to pay back with interest hanging over you.

2. Reduces the Need for Credit

Having a Rainy-Day Fund lessens the need to take out loans, overdrafts and other forms of credit – credit that becomes debt. These money suckers hang like millstones around your neck and drain your resources. Paying interest only soaks up more of your money, money that is better spent on the good things in life and not on wasteful interest payments. The more debt you carry, the more vulnerable to economic change like a job loss you are. Whether you have a job or not, if you have obligations they need to be met. The less debt you carry, the freer you are to make choices because you want to, not because you have to.

3. Reduces Stress

Without a Rainy-Day Fund, a sudden expense like the car breaking down turns into a stressful catastrophe. The only option might be to borrow money. Borrowed money never comes for free. Extra payments mean extra debt, which has caused many a sleepless night. The worry of meeting repayments on an already stretched budget can be a profound source of anxiety, especially if several surprise expenses happen all at once.

4. Reduces the Cost of Living

Having a Rainy-Day Fund to draw on can make all the difference when it comes to replacing larger, expensive items like washing machines and other appliances. It gives you the option to buy better-quality items that have superior warranties, better safety records and that you are less likely to run into issues with down the line. There can be a false economy with buying cheaper, as it might not stand the test of time and ultimately cost more in maintenance or just not be as safe or effective.

If less money is spent on maintenance, upgrading or loan repayments, a more significant portion of what you're earning is yours to keep. Outgoings become more manageable, as there are fewer demands on your salary.

5. Let's You Take Advantage of Opportunities

Having a sizeable Rainy-Day Fund allows you to take advantage of opportunities. When I say opportunities, I don't mean that great holiday deal. I am talking here about finding the perfect home and locking it in at a reasonable price with a bigger deposit and lower mortgage. A healthy Rainy-Day Fund can help you buy a car for cash and avoid being burdened with financing.

It must be noted here that taking advantage of larger opportunities like this should only be done in addition to taking care of the rainy-day basics first. The core purpose of a Rainy-Day Fund is to protect you from the impact of medium-term issues – life's smaller but detrimental surprises. Money to weather a rainy day should never be used for anything other than predefined events. However, once the Rainy-Day Fund has been adequately shored up, any additional money can be stored here too, to take advantage of life's other opportunities.

6. Makes Long-Term Saving Possible

Think ahead a few years and figure out what substantial expenses are on the horizon, whether it's a home, car or college. The earlier you get started on that saving, the easier it will be. Having a large Rainy-Day Fund will allow you to cover life's smaller surprises. Once they are accounted for, any other money can be put aside for the long-term things. Knowing you have the safety net to cover that broken-down appliance or extra car tyres means that you know the momentum you have for saving for the longer-term things doesn't get interfered with.

How to Build a Rainy-Day Fund

A Rainy-Day Fund is most definitely a Pay Yourself First item. If you are serious about getting out of the debt cycle and building a life of your design, then creating one of these is a key priority. The Rainy-Day Fund needs to be one of the first bills every month.

Start small and build. We are all human; we like the quick win. As such, it is easier to save more when the short-term goal is set. For example, committing to saving up for a €500 Rainy-Day Fund is doable compared to a €10,000 one, particularly if you are new to saving. Once the €500 goal is reached, you have proven you can do it. You can then aim to save €1,000. Then save another, and then another, until you have a good-sized rainy-day cushion.

BE PATIENT, DON'T GET DISHEARTENED

If you are just starting on your Rainy-Day Fund habit, build it steadily. Most of us are not in a position to create a large Rainy-Day Fund overnight. Pensions and other savings will also be vying for a share of the Pay Yourself First money. It is important here to not get stressed out and divide out the money as fairly as you can, depending on your current priorities. Another thing with life is that you may need to draw on your Rainy-Day Fund before it gets a chance to reach its full amount. Unexpected expenses don't have a schedule and most often arrive unannounced. Having even a small amount of money to hand to fix the problem, rather than resorting to a loan or credit, is a marked improvement. Just use what is in the account to get you through the problem and then start again. The amount of money that you have already diligently saved is already making your life easier by being there to draw on.

If you find that it takes longer than expected to build this fund, it does not matter. What matters is that you start and stay consistent. Grit your teeth and stick with it. Be proud of every addition to that fund. You are taking back control one euro at a time.

HOW MUCH SHOULD BE IN A RAINY-DAY FUND?

The size of a Rainy-Day Fund will depend on where you are in life and what you need. A young single person starting out in life won't need as big a fund as a married person with children. A homeowner will need a larger fund than someone renting. Car owners will need more than cyclists. Whatever the amount, it is specific to you and your life.

Grab a pen and paper. Take the time to work through what could go wrong. Calculate how much it would cost to fix or replace the things you need to meet your responsibilities. Include things like large appliances, car maintenance or a job loss. If all these things happened at the same time, how much would it set you back? Figure out this worst-case scenario and add an extra 10 per cent. That is your magic number.

I've read many recommendations about having somewhere between three to six months' worth of income saved as a Rainy-Day Fund. This is a good number to aim for if you are not sure how much you need. However, if that seems like too big a challenge, then, as mentioned earlier, start small. Having a little Rainy-Day Fund is infinitely better than not having one at all.

THE RULES OF A RAINY-DAY FUND

A Rainy-Day Fund exists solely to fix, repair or replace necessary items in your life. It is for the things that must be attended to in order to get normality back on track. Understanding and sticking to the rules will ensure that it is there when you need it.

What Is It Used For?

* Repairs: the washing machine needs fixing, or the car needs extra work.
* Income change: If you suddenly find yourself unemployed or your income has dropped, and there is a gap, use it to make ends meet until you are back on your feet again.
* Replacements: If you know that you will need a new fridge or work done on your house, this is where you store the money until it is required.

What Is It Not Used for?

* If you are tired and want a take-away, look elsewhere.
* If you have a night out and nothing to wear, this is not your spending pot. Recheck your wardrobe, ring a friend or go to a thrift store.
* If the grocery budget is maxed out and you want something tasty – go back to the fridge and lower your standards.
* If you decide that you need a newer, bigger TV, save up and buy it when you can afford to buy it with cash, and not a moment earlier.

In short, this fund is not for wants, this is a place to store resources for needs. This money that you have worked hard to put aside should not be dipped into on a whim. Don't devalue it by depleting it to buy things that don't matter. Spends from a Rainy-Day Fund have to make your life better and bring value to you.

A REAL-LIFE EXAMPLE

Not long ago our only car was a beat-up 2010 estate. Many of our appliances had seen better days, and both of us were considering further education. As homeowners and parents, we knew there were other expenses on the horizon. These were known entities and, thanks to the

Rainy-Day Fund, had been planned and saved for. It took a long while to build the fund up to where we needed it to be, but eventually we got there. There were times during the funding when I thought we had enough, as surely we would never need that much in one go, but we persisted and eventually reached our target.

It Rained

Within a couple of months of my stepping back from work to embark on the No-Spend Year the car died, college fees came due, and we had to replace two large appliances. These things wiped out the Rainy-Day Fund in no time. It was a whirlwind of major expenses, one after another. It was stressful but thankfully the stress had nothing to do with money and we were able to handle it.

I dread to think what would have happened if it hadn't been there to draw on. My best guess is that I would have had to go back to my job and my husband would have lost his place on the course. The kids would have gone back to their childminder, and the stress would have been piled back on again. All the work that we had done to create a healthier work–life balance would have been for nothing, and I would have been back on my early morning commute, missing the children and pining for a different life. Having the cash there made everything workable. This is the power of a Rainy-Day Fund and mindful spending habit.

SUMMARY

A Rainy-Day Fund will reduce stress, allow for better decision-making, helps plan for future events and lessens the chances of drawing down more debt. The Rainy-Day Fund is an appropriate name when it comes to mindful spending. Having one allows a person to have more choice and flexibility when it comes to spending during the moments when life blindsides us. It is not a matter of if, but when. Rainy-Day Funds have saved me on more than one occasion and have made hard times more manageable than they would otherwise have been. I might not have ever written this book if it wasn't for our Rainy-Day Fund keeping our heads above water. I'll let you have your own opinion on that.

15

HABIT 3: MINDFUL CASHFLOW

A mindful cashflow is a document where all incomes and outgoings are recorded. Mindful cashflows are about channelling your money in the direction of your choosing. Like a riverbank guides water to the sea, a cashflow directs your money to its best destination. It focuses on leading and optimising, rather than cutbacks and deprivation. Cashflows provide full transparency regarding where your money is going. This knowledge allows you to make the changes required to stem wasteful leaks and channel that newfound cash towards things that make a positive difference. Once a good cashflow is in place, little maintenance is needed, and the return on time spent is enormous.

The driving force behind starting one is often emotional discomfort or pain caused by expenses that overwhelm your income. Maybe you start tracking your money due to emotional upheaval and maintained the practice because you realised how doing so could benefit your life. You may be one of the lucky few raised with sound financial practices and a healthy money mindset. You may understand how important having a cashflow is because you know it helps you to achieve your goals. On the flip side, you may have never adopted a tracking system because your spending hasn't caused you any apparent problems. Some may never need to use a cashflow due to high incomes. They can spend how they please today and still blissfully pursue tomorrow. However, these lucky people are very few and far between.

WHERE DID THE TRADITIONAL BUDGET GO WRONG?

Budgeting is often a starting point in many personal finance journeys. In the past, the budgeting torch may have been picked up because of low income, high expenses, or a debt epiphany. Maybe an unexpectedly large bill brought the financial cliff edge on which you stood into sharp focus. Perhaps you wanted to live on one income so one parent could stay home, the reason matters little.

Many are turned off by the word 'budget', as it is a term loaded with negative connotations. Budgets have a terrible reputation, mainly because most budgets are ill-conceived, poorly adhered to and viewed with resentment. They are associated with frugality, deprivation and a less enjoyable life. However, a budget is not in itself a bad thing. It is an immensely powerful tool that will cast light on every cent of your money and track where it is going. Many people have had massive success with traditional budgeting. Unfortunately, this cannot be said for the vast majority of us. Whether you choose to use the term 'budget' or 'cashflow' is entirely up to your personal preference. However, what I am looking for is a decision to leave behind the disagreeable nature of deprivation and frugality associated with tracking expenses. Instead I want you to embrace the power and freedom that comes with being the shepherd of your money and you future

WHY A MINDFUL CASHFLOW IS SO POWERFUL

Before we start, I need a commitment. I need you to stop thinking about tracking your money as bad, or restrictive. Instead, think of it as a smart way to find and direct your money where it needs to go. A cashflow is a tool that will turn your wallet from a sieve into a beautiful system that effortlessly guides your money to places that will make your life easier, less stressful and, dare I say, more fun.

Whatever your history with money, a mindful cashflow will help you live a happier, more fulfilled life. Using a cashflow is particularly valuable in the early stages of getting your money together. It gathers all your information about your money on one sheet and makes it easier to see where there are leaks that need to be plugged, and where improvements can be made. Mindful spending is spending with purpose and the cashflow records it happening.

How to Create a Mindful Cashflow

1. Determine Your Income

Grab a piece of paper, open an Excel document, Google spreadsheet or whatever your preferred medium is. This is your new cashflow. It doesn't have to be flashy, it just has to be honest and accurate. Calculate your income from every source. Any money coming to you each week or month must be noted and totalled up. A regular salary is straightforward. However, it is just as essential to include benefits, maintenance, dividends, rental income and money from side hustles. The more accurate the number, the clearer and more effective your cash flow will be. List these at the top of your weekly/monthly cashflow. Add up all the income and find the total.

2. Pay Yourself First

Pay Yourself First is the first port of call for every good mindful cashflow. This must be the first bill each payday and the first bill in your cashflow without exception. There is no upper limit to the amount saved in this category, but the more money dedicated to this section, the more worthwhile your work will have been

The Pay Yourself First section sits right below the income section to remind you that this is the first and most important bill of the month. Initially, this might be the last space filled in accurately as it is important to understand your expense level so you can determine how much it is possible to save. The aim is to increase the numbers in this first category over time, as unnecessary spends are curbed or eliminated. Every euro needs a job, so as soon as money is freed up from going towards paying off debt or other past costs, it needs to be assigned to building your life. And that is the Pay Yourself First Section.

3. List All of Your Outgoings

It is just as important to be honest here as elsewhere. Take the time to go through old bank statements and receipts, ensuring you note all expenses, both regular and sporadic. A missed bill at this point can put a real spanner in the works and throw the month or quarter out entirely. When it comes to outgoings there are two main categories, fixed and discretionary. Fixed expenses are listed beneath Pay Yourself First, as they are usually the non-negotiable costs, such as accommodation, electricity, heating, broadband and other regular bills. Once these are accounted for add them up and find out what the total for these essential bills comes to.

Once all the fixed bills have been added up, do the same for discretionary spending. This can be a little more difficult, as discretionary spends tend to vary more. However, I would advise you to keep things simple here. There is no need for hundreds of categories and heavily detailed breakdowns. A few simple line items will suffice, for example, grocery, fuel, entertainment, presents, household goods, pets, fun, etc. To find an accurate number for these expenses, go back to your bank statements and add up all these expenses over a six- to twelve-month period. This will give you an average of what your monthly costs are. This can take a while, but it is critical that you do it. Calculating exactly what you have spent historically will give you a good indication of what future costs will look like. Add these up to get a picture of where your money is really going.

If you determine that you are spending more than you are making, then it is time to do some cutting. Being able to save will ensure that you don't go further into debt. The best way to figure out where you can cut down expenses is to track your spending and record every outgoing for a month. Seemingly insignificant items, such as a cup of coffee or a snack, add up over time. Spending just €5 a day on coffee or snacks adds up to a massive €1,825 per year. This sort of money can make a difference in your life.

Make sure that fun money is included, along with amounts for holidays, clothes and other forms of entertainment. Unless you are planning to have a No-Spend Year as I did, these are legitimate and real expenses that drain your income just like any other. Being prepared for them will allow you to manage them carefully without throwing your numbers out completely.

4. Keep Yourself Accountable

Accountability is king or queen – take your pick, just understand how important accountability is. From the outset, schedule time every few days to update your cashflow. Inputting expenses regularly increases awareness of costs and lessens the likelihood of you splurging without thinking. The other side of this coin is you get to enjoy the satisfying feeling of reaching a savings goal or eliminating a debt.

5. Lean into Your Mindful Cash Flow to Make Savings

Now that you know your numbers, it is time to get them working for you and not the other way around. If you've always thought you were too busy to take the time to shop around utility providers, now is your time. Put down the remote control and get comparing. Switching is easy nowadays; most of it can be done online, whether it's your phone, broadband, electricity, TV or gas. This is the time to look at your costs and get clever about them. No one cares whether you pay top rate for your electricity or not. However, changing provider every year can rack up enough savings to enable you to upgrade your car with ease when the time comes.

Look at all your direct debits and subscription payments, check to see if you are out of contract and compare with other providers, with a view to moving to one that offers better value. You'll be amazed at the savings that can be made. Savings that can be put to work lowering debt or adding to that Rainy-Day Fund.

When it comes to food and other discretionary outgoing, these are ones that you have a lot of control over, probably more that you realise. Set yourself a weekly or monthly food budget and stick to it. Think laterally about gifts, socialising and clothes, as there are so many ways to enjoy life now without it costing your future.

6. Be Practical and Realistic and Pace Yourself

Just like a child learning to walk, eat or read, it takes time. Give yourself the same time and compassion as you would anyone who is grasping a new concept. Do not expect the first month or even the first few months to go smoothly. However, understand that, as time goes by, you will get more competent and proficient. Money is a long game. Once you are optimising savings and reducing debt, you are moving forward no matter how slow progress may seem. Keep to your own pace, not anyone else's. Allow the cashflow journey to be flexible and don't beat yourself up if one area of your budget goes over. Simply re-jig your numbers for that month and try to improve for the next month. No one gets it right the first time.

PULLING IT ALL TOGETHER

Once all the numbers have been tabulated, you will get a clear picture of where you are financially. For some, it will be a shock, but for others, it may come as a pleasant surprise. The main thing here is that you have a starting point: you have direction and clarity. Use this as a compass to guide your money where it needs to go.

Keep flexibility in your cashflow, particularly at the start, and don't beat yourself up if it doesn't work perfectly the first time around. Everything worthwhile takes time. It'll take time to really understand all your spending habits. However, if you follow these steps and view your cashflow as your companion on your path to freedom, then I can assure you that you will reach whatever goal you set yourself.

THE BENEFITS OF A MINDFUL CASHFLOW

A mindful cashflow is a plan that prioritises mindful spending. Priorities will vary from person to person. It may be to get out of debt, save for a home, college or to pay off the mortgage early. Your cashflow is the road map. It gives transparency to all your outgoings and incomings.

Without a cashflow, how do you know where the money is going? If you drift aimlessly through the month hoping there is enough in the account to last until payday, you are unlikely to build anything worthwhile. Without one, how can you know what your expenses are, relative to your income, and how can you ever get that house deposit, that trip of a lifetime or that much-needed car?

It is only by knowing where every euro of your money is going each month and making a plan that you can make things happen. A cashflow helps you figure out your long-term goals and tracks them as you work towards them. It won't stop you wanting that chic sparkling dress, but it will make you pause and remind you that you're working on something so much bigger and more critical. Knowing this will make it easier to turn around and walk out of the store empty-handed.

Mindful cashflows stops you spending money you don't have. Before the widespread use of credit cards, you could tell if you were living within your means. It was simple – if there was money left in your account after paying all your bills, then you obviously were. However, in our credit-riddled society, this has become an increasingly grey area.

A cashflow categorises your money. It makes it clear where the money is spent. This allows you to then gauge if a particular area is sucking up your money or, alternatively, not getting enough attention. For example, if the socialising column is looking high and the savings column has cobwebs, then there might be a need for a bit of rebalancing. It reveals areas where you're spending too much money and helps you refocus on your most important goals. Following a realistic cashflow frees up spare cash so you can use your money on the things that really matter to you instead of frittering it away on things you don't even remember buying.

We have been trained to overspend and enticed into buying things that are just plain unnecessary. Segmenting your money in a cashflow will show you exactly how much is spent where and will give you a starting point to make those ·changes. It creates a lovely system that shows you how much you earn, how much you can afford to spend each month and how much you need to save.

If you think that filling out a spreadsheet and keeping track of a cashflow isn't nearly as much fun as going on a shameless shopping spree, just give it a try and see how good you feel when you have succeeded at the end of the month. Wouldn't it be much more satisfying to end your month stress-free and a little wealthier, and not worrying about how you are going to pay off that credit card? It puts you in control of your money, rather than letting your money control you. If you feel like you are not in control of your money and you are always wondering where it went and what happened to it, putting it all in black and white on a cashflow helps.

Setting out expenses at the beginning of the month makes it easier to manage your money. Checking in each day or week helps you monitor how you're getting on and prevents overspending. You can make clear and logical decisions at any time, knowing you have all the information in one place.

We have discussed the importance of a Rainy-Day Fund. Life is filled with unexpected surprises, some good and some not so good. The Rainy-Day Fund helps you deal with the not-so-good ones: if you lose your job, become sick or injured, if the heating goes or the car breaks down. These can all lead to severe financial turmoil. People with a cashflow tend to save more money and have a Rainy-Day Fund. The reason for this is straightforward: if you lay all your income and expenditure out, you can see clearly where you are and how often these 'surprises' occur. It turns out that things go wrong more often than we'd like to think.

Knowing your expenses will let you spot the unnecessary ones and curb or eliminate them from your cashflow altogether. Perhaps there is a subscription you don't use or had forgotten about. Cancelling it loosens up that money for savings or debt paydown. It transforms hidden expenses into growing assets. As in any other situation, if you know all the facts it is easier to create a good outcome. Knowledge is power.

It sheds light on bad spending habits. It might seem hard at first but, compiling a cashflow forces you to take a closer look at spending habits. You may notice that you're forking out for things you don't need. Do you honestly watch all 300 channels, or need 30 pairs of black shoes and takeaways four nights a week? Using a cashflow allows you to rethink your spending habits, adjust where your money is going and channel money away from those bad habits and refocus it on your dreams.

It also allows you to be flexible with your money. Life throws things at us all the time and your cashflow can reflect that. When the numbers are set out at the beginning of the month, you could, as the days unfold, move money between the categories. If, for example, you've been invited to a birthday party unexpectedly and you really want to go, you could eat out less or wear an old outfit again that month to compensate.

Money can be moved between categories as needed. Avoid touching cash from savings and always pay our bills, but otherwise adjust the remaining columns as you go. Learn what makes your budget work for you. Following the rules of never dipping into savings will not only save you from over-spending, it will also teach you how to live within your means. Over time you'll learn to recognise triggers and adjust your discretionary income to accommodate this, so that the money lasts until the end of the pay period.

A huge bonus of having a cashflow is that it helps you sleep better at night. Knowing where your money is and guiding it to where it needs to go protects you from having to worry about how you're going to make ends meet. So many people lose sleep over financial issues, not knowing if there is enough money to pay the bills or deal with upcoming expenses. This can really take its toll on the body. When you cashflow your money wisely, you'll never lose sleep over financial issues again. It is such a source of comfort.

Cashflows play their part in building good relationships, too. A good cashflow is not just a spending plan; it's a communication tool. The transparency provided by a cashflow can bring a couple closer together by working towards common goals and reducing arguments about money. Once both parties can see what is happening with the income, it is much easier to create empathy for each other and build a path that works.

THE THEORY OF THE ID, THE KEY TO A SUCCESSFUL CASHFLOW

I thought that it was important to give the Id a section of its own. This little guy has been the ruination of many good cashflows and has scuppered so many good intentions that it would make you cry to count them. Understanding the Id when it comes to managing money is a big factor in making your money work for you.

When it comes making a cashflow work for the long term, it is essential to factor in not only flexibility but also fun money. Fun money, just as the name suggests, is for fun. It is to be spent as you want to, guilt-free, no consequences. Whether it's for nights out, clothes or twenty take-away cups of coffee is an entirely personal choice. Fun money is a set amount that you put aside to have fun with each pay period, and what you do with it is up to you.

However, it must be spent, not saved or used for someone else, it is entirely for the frivolous things in life. Whatever the amount is must be consumed up to that amount, and not a cent more. This is important for several reasons. We have to live and enjoy our lives today, as well as saving for the future. Doing only one at a time won't work, finding a balance between living now and saving is the only way.

The best way that I have found to describe the importance of fun money is through the theory of the founder of psychoanalysis, Sigmund Freud. Freud was not known for his budgeting prowess but I feel that his theory of the Id goes a long way toward helping us understand how we interact with our money and making sense of some of the poor financial decisions we make. Once we understand why they are made, we can figure out ways to avoid making them and to keep a budget on track.

Freud described the psyche as being composed of three distinct interacting parts: the Id (the child), the Ego (the mediator) and the Superego (the cop). These three parts of the mind interact with each other and the results determine how we react to specific scenarios, even if those actions don't always make sense. Freud described the personality as an iceberg. The tip of the iceberg represents our conscious awareness and the part under the water represents our unconscious mind. Our unconscious mind is where all our hidden desires, memories and thoughts reside.

The Id resides in the unconscious and is the child-like, instinctual part. It is the only part of the psyche that exists at birth and is the dominant force of the personality. When a child is born, it is driven solely by its basic needs to eat, drink, sleep and be held. The Id motivates actions related to immediate gratification, it only searches out pleasure. From birth, that pleasure is the comfort found in eating, sleeping and being held. The Id also controls all life and death instincts. This drive for immediate gratification often manifests as a stroppy, bold child that wants to follow its desires and is willing to cause trouble to get it. The Id does not change as we grow. Instead, we develop coping mechanisms as we grow up to fit in with society and develop other parts of the personality to manage and counterbalance the unpredictable Id. These separate parts allow us to deal with the Id in socially acceptable ways.

The Superego, for example, is the part that comprises our internal morals and values. The Superego will continuously push us to be a better, more virtuous and ethical version of ourselves. It's like a cop, ensuring that social laws are adhered so. The Ego is the part that mediates between the Id and Superego. The Ego must find a balance between the urges of the Id, the virtuosity of the Superego and the demands of reality. When each is kept in balance, things go right. It is easier to stay on track, and goals become attainable.

FREUD APPLIED TO LIFE

Many of you will be familiar with the high failure rate of New Year's resolutions. Specifically, those related to getting fitter and healthier. The Superego is in its element here, cheering you on to be a better version of yourself. It does an excellent job for a while of keeping you on track and ticking all the boxes. The new you is just around the corner. It works so hard to help you be this ideal version of yourself.

Meanwhile, the Id isn't getting a word in, and is not happy. Unfortunately, very soon the Id makes itself heard and trips you up the first chance it gets. You bypass the healthy fridge and dial the local take-away, ordering seventeen pizzas and scoffing down ice-cream for dessert. The Id is now sated, happy that its need for pleasure was met. All the Id wants is to indulge the impulse to find pleasure all the time. It wants its desires and urges to be satisfied immediately and that happens with alarming success. Disheartened, you fling the trainers into the corner to gather dust with all your other good intentions. According to the Id, balance is restored. That is, it got to be the winner, defeating its opposite, the Superego. The power struggle begins again as the Ego strives to find a healthy balance between to two.

FREUD ON CASHFLOW

A similar process often happens in traditional cashflows. You diligently draw one up, full of the best intentions and goodwill. Large amounts are allocated to savings, without fully understanding or taming the outgoings. Little is left for flexibility, and nothing is left for fun, impulse buys or entertainment. You think that you are going to whip yourself into financial shape and believe that going cold turkey on fun is the only way. The Superego is in its element, revelling in this new, structured way of being. Until, inevitably, the Id comes crashing in, and blows the whole lot sky-high in one big spending spree, leaving most of us to declare how terrible we are with money and feeling utterly disillusioned.

However, including fun money in the monthly cashflow allows the Id to have its fun without throwing a wrecking ball into our savings. Building flexibility into the cashflow relieves the feeling of deprivation, and suddenly everything becomes more manageable. By regularly allowing yourself to spend a small amount of money frivolously, and being realistic with savings, you should be able to make cashflow work, and work well.

Each month, allocate a set amount for discretionary, fun spending. Money to buy as many coffees, meals out, clothes and trips to the salon as you want, as long as it doesn't exceed the amount designated. That is the only rule.

Don't feel guilty about having beautiful things; living a full life includes a bit of indulgence. Once it stays within the predetermined limits, these indulgences can be relished. The fun money allows the Id to have its time to play while leaving the Superego to save in peace.

AN IMPERFECT CASHFLOW WORKS

The mind is not a binary thing, so allowing flexibility is important to success. Building pressure valves into it is essential. A cashflow must not be too rigid, because if it is you will snap and most probably fail. Understand that letting off steam is a good thing. Build it into the plan and then the chances of a successful outcome suddenly rise significantly.

SUMMARY

A mindful cashflow is a tool for tracking money successfully in a transparent and results-driven way. It helps to find where you are leaking money and can help plug the holes and divert the money in the direction of your choosing. Having all your incomings and outgoings in one place can prevent you from dipping into savings. It takes the stress out of spending because you know what you have to spend and what is earmarked for other things. It frees up bandwidth that is needed for making the right buying decisions.

Choice and freedom are the true Holy Grails of life. Not only can a cashflow help you build towards this, but it can also become one of the most fun games that you will ever play – a game where you can really and truly be the winner in life. Every goal, aim, plan and journey starts with building a robust cashflow. Whether it's a paper-based cashflow over software versions, or using a card over cash, make it personal to you. Find out which method is best and go with it. Budgeting is a very personal thing, and if what you're doing is not working for you, change it up.

Whatever form your cashflow takes, it should be simple, easy to update and always live and up to date. A mindful cashflow is only as good as the effort you put into keeping it accurate. You can simplify the process by using percentages of your income to cover your set expenses, savings amounts, and your spending money and then simply track the money as it is spent. This means fewer categories and a lot more flexibility.

If you have found yourself failing in the money department, cut yourself some slack. Allow your Id some room to play. Once the little mischief-maker is given his sandbox to play in, the Superego can cheer you on while you are building that future you have always dreamed of. This is the balance between enjoying your life now and protecting your future. You may decide that an envelope system suits you best, particularly for the discretionary section of the cashflow. The benefit of this is that it eliminates the need to track little individual spends. What you have for a category is in the envelope, so it is up to you how and when you spend it within that category, but once it's gone, it's gone until next pay period.

The main thing to remember when creating your cashflow is this: it is your money and your cashflow. It must be malleable and must correspond to your values and not anyone else's. If you want to put a large portion of your money towards hobbies and other leisure activities, that is your prerogative. As long as Pay Yourself First saving goals and essential bill commitments are met, what you choose to do with the rest of your money is up to you. Mindful Cashflow is not about limiting the fun in your life but opening it up to opportunities and making your money work harder, so that over the long term you don't have to.

16

HABIT 4: NO-SPEND DAYS

A No-Spend Day is one of the best ways to put mindful spending into action. These days supercharge the mental muscle you need to make healthy money habits an ingrained part of your life. They are one of the most effective ways to slow impulse spending and find money that you never knew you had. Impulse spending is responsible for many euros being mindlessly spent over a year and multiple more times over a lifetime. Understanding the importance of managing the small spends makes all the difference between successfully saving or diving further into debt.

We have all been fooled into thinking that taking care of small amounts of money won't make a difference. I will show you that this is not true. Managing small spends can make dreams happen. No-Spend Days are like magic; they compound lots of small, seemingly inconsequential spends and roll them into something worthwhile. Saving money is not always about income; what a person does with that income is just as important.

WHAT IS A NO-SPEND DAY?

Simply put, a No-Spend Day is any day where no money is spent other than on essential bills and groceries. We all need to eat and keep a roof over our heads. We need electricity, a warm home, and a full belly. It is for this reason that essential bills like accommodation, electricity, broadband and groceries are not taken into consideration when it comes to calculating a No-Spend Day.

Cutting back excessively on essential items leads to deprivation and a loss of quality of life. That is against the nature of mindful spending and is unsustainable. Mindful spending is about abundance and the creation of happiness in life. Therefore, care should be taken to avoid cutting essential spending back so far that these are impacted. No-Spend Days are not designed to penalise; they are intended to curb wasteful spending so that you have the money to live that great life.

For a day to be classed as a No-Spend Day, essential bills and grocery shopping are where spending must stop. Any expenses outside these categories are classed as wants and not needs. Money spent on anything other than a necessity causes the day to be classed as a Spend Day.

Spend Days are days where money is spent on things over and above the essential needs list above. Take-away coffee, restaurant lunches, clothes, shoes or other expenses would fall into this Spend Day category. That also includes things like food deliveries, makeup and gadgets, and sales where another white shirt is purchased even though there are six near-identical white shirts in the closet. Meals out, coffee mornings with cream buns, cinema trips, magazines and subscriptions that don't get used ... the list of things to spend on is infinite, and there are many with a vested interest in helping us part with our hard-earned money.

SPEND DAYS ARE OK

Spending is a part of living. Hence, Spend Days are not a bad thing; they are a normal part of life and should be enjoyed. There are times when clothes are needed, the car needs work, or the only place to meet a friend is in a cafe. There are also times when it is nice to check out a new restaurant or the latest blockbuster. These are things that add icing to the cake of life and should be enjoyed to the full. These are ideal fun money spends.

The trouble happens when the number of Spend Days and the amount of money spent on those days makes money tight. If eating out is normal and not a treat, or the wardrobe is brimming with clothes that have hardly been worn, or you can't remember how or when the money was spent, there is a problem. Additionally, if these purchases were made because we're tired, feeling lazy, impulsive or emotional, or if you are eyeing up the credit card to get you through until the end of the month, then Spend Days are out of control.

If this is the case, you are doing yourself a massive disservice. Especially if the Pay Yourself First habit and the Rainy-Day Fund are not in place. If this is the case, this disservice is costing you dearly.

How to Start a No-Spend Day Habit

If it is your first time trying a No-Spend Day, it is important not to overthink it. Instead, make it into a game, a fun game. Watch your habits and try to identify what triggers spending. Everyone is different, but if you can understand why you spend money, then it can be easier to put a plan in place to slow this spending down.

Begin with just one No-Spend Day a week. Get a calendar and tick off the No-Spend Days as you have them. If that is successful, try two a week and keep it at that level for a while. Continue this way until you find what is optimal for you. There is no right or wrong number of No-Spend Days to have, the important thing is to keep trying to have them. Plan ahead and find a balance between doing the things that you really love and enjoying them versus keeping that purse shut tight because you have better things to do with your money.

Simple Steps to a No-Spend Day

Pick a day to have as your first No-Spend Day. First aim for a weekday. These days tend to have more structure and it's generally easier to avoid temptation. Starting this practice on a weekend can be a bit more of a challenge

1. If you are tempted to spend money, pause and think about what you're wanting to spend money on. Switch off the autopilot and be in the moment. It is time to really consider what value this transaction is bringing to your life.
2. Take three deep breaths.
3. Think about how this investment will affect areas of your life such as health, relationships, purpose, culture, creativity or money. The more parts it beneficially affects, the happier you will be with the transaction.
4. Ask yourself:
    *   Is this something you could live without?
    *   Is there a way to do this and get the same or a better result at a lower cost?
    *   Can you share the cost with someone to lower it and spread more happiness?
5. After thinking about the above steps, will you make a new choice?
6. Be mindful about what you've learned and how you felt about the decision.
7. Harness the feeling derived from each decision to build new mindful spending habits.

TIPS TO MAKE A NO-SPEND DAY EASY

- Make a packed lunch (a nice one, one you want to eat).
- Bring snacks too (make sure these are nice, too).
- Make your coffee at home and bring it in a travel mug.
- Avoid shopping centres, go for a walk in a park or outdoors instead.
- Invite a friend to your place for coffee instead of meeting at a cafe.
- Invite friends to dinner at yours instead of having a meal out.
- Go to a public park instead of an indoor playcentre with the kids.
- Check out local groups and social media sites like Facebook for things that are happening in your local area.
- Look out for festivals, community events, the local library, tourist office and Eventbrite for free events. You'll be surprised at what fun things might be going on in your locality.
- Unsubscribe from retail websites and store newsletters. You can always resubscribe; they will take you back if you really want to rejoin, I'm sure.
- Start a project that you've been meaning to get to.
- Look around your home and get some maintenance done, clothes mended or a meal cooked and try to up-skill.
- Learn a new skill. There is so much free information online; almost any skill can be learned for free if you are willing to do the research.
- Ireland is littered with ancient monuments, castles and trails for hikes and walks, many of which are free to the public. Get some fresh air into those lungs.

THE BENEFITS OF A NO-SPEND DAY

The benefits of a No-Spend Day are many when it comes to your financial wellbeing, but here are just a few of the more obvious ones.

1. Your Time

Practising No-Spend Days increases the respect and value that you place on the days spent working to earn that income. The savings made from these days over time will give you more freedom in the future.

2. Curbs Unnecessary Spending

A No-Spend Day puts mindfulness into spending decisions. They encourage a person to pause and think, 'Do I really need this?' before the wallet is opened. It helps when planning the day ahead and lends itself to a more organised life.

3. Will Train You to Look for Value

No-Spend Days enhance mindful spending. They put a buffer between you and the fancy advertising. When money is spent, it is with purpose and not on a whim. Falling into lousy spending habits puts you at risk. Mindless spending, on the other hand, puts you at risk of trading long commutes and years of your life spent away from your family for a wardrobe full of clothes and lunches out that you'll never remember. Your life is worth more than that.

4. Allows Easier Tracking of Spends

Tracking spending can be tedious at times. If the number of transactions in a week or month is limited it is easier to track spending and understand where your hard-earned money is going.

5. Redirects Money

Money that would otherwise be mindlessly frittered away on things that you'll have forgotten a day later can now be put towards things that make a positive difference. This extra money helps to pay off debt faster, increase savings and shore up Rainy-Day Funds. These days accelerate time to money goals, which provides an increased feeling of security.

6. No-Spend Days Feel Fantastic

No-Spend Days are not about hiding away and waiting for it to be over, they are about finding ways to enjoy yourself without resorting to the crutch of spending money as entertainment. There is a sense of achievement around completing a No-Spend Day. Ticking it off the calendar after a successful day of no spending is a satisfying sensation. One that can be repeated as often as desired. Keeping track of No-Spend Days and trying to beat a personal best week after week and month after month can become quite a fun game.

7. Makes Your Money More Meaningful

Once this habit is in place, automatic mindless spending becomes a thing of the past. The value derived from a transaction is thought about on a deeper level. The result is that when money is spent, it feels good and worthwhile.

SUMMARY

A No-Spend Day is a simple tool that is easily applied. It is a great way to get ahead with money. It helps to find money that you never knew you had. It is wealth born out of thousands of tiny decisions made daily. Small actions like bringing coffee to work rather than buying a take-away one or cooking at home instead of getting takeout all add up. They may appear inconsequential, but over time these positive steps forward add up to big jumps that will build your security.

A No-Spend Day does not have to be a day where you hide under the duvet and pray for the next morning. Make it something to look forward to, invite friends over, cook at home, and plan free activities, a free festival or event, game night, movie night, or trip to the park. Make it part of your lifestyle, build No-Spend Days into your week. Make a game of it. It'll open your eyes to many new activities, pastimes and ideas that may not have manifested otherwise.

Making a habit of having No-Spend Days creates greater confidence when it comes to managing your money. They give greater transparency about where your money is going and rewire you to look for options and fun things to do in life that don't cost money.

Try one and see how good it feels.

17

HABIT 5: USE MINDFULLY

U se mindfully focuses on what you already own and aims to get the best out of those things. It takes day-to-day consumables like beauty and cleaning products and enlists them to play their part in building a secure life. Seemingly insignificant household consumables are often overlooked when it comes to saving money. However, I can assure you that they hold their own when it comes to getting the best out of your money.

WHY DOESN'T COMMERCIALISM WORK IN YOUR FAVOUR?

The advent of modernity, with all its convenience and choice, has changed everything about how we shop. Commercialism introduced a wide range of products, options and choices we never had before. New gadgets appear every day, each shinier and more tempting than the last. Anything we desire is at our fingertips, all we have to do is click and pay. We can drink water from far-off countries and wash our hair with exotic herbs procured from the depths of mystical jungles. We have a choice of 157 different styles of mid-blue jeans. These were a fantasy only a couple of decades ago. Now, it is normal.

Having beautiful things is enjoyable, life is to be enjoyed. Unfortunately, many of us have hit a point where we are drowning in our own stuff. Overwhelm kicks in, clutter fills cabinets, lotions are stacked on shelves and bottles of shampoo line the shower. Drawers are brimming with scrubs, masks and scents that we intend to get around to using but never do. Yet we buy more, more products that never get used. In the end, we are buried under a mountain of our own impulse purchases, often wondering how we are going to make it to payday as we skate dangerously close to the overdraft limit. But hey, at least we have enough shampoo to last us until the next century. The things that we thought would make us more in truth just make us less. All the excess products do is lighten our pockets and suffocate us.

We are not wittier, superior, more intelligent or likeable for having multiples of things clogging up our precious cupboards. We are still ourselves, just with more stuff and less money. The marketing promise to fix that pressing problem in our life is generally left unfulfilled. Empty promises stare back from the bathroom shelves, which brimming with packets of things we forget we own. We fall for the unmissable deal, fantastic sale price or shiny new packaging.

'But we are worth it!' I hear you cry. At least that is what we have been told. Wrong. I am going to correct that mantra here and now. The truth is this: You are worth so much more than that.

WHY USE MINDFULLY?

Marketing is hard to resist; it never tells you that you have enough, it always tells you that you need more. We are led to think we are smart for stocking up when that promotion comes around. In theory, this thinking is sound, and there are times when it can work to our advantage. However, the problem occurs when, the following week, we spy a better deal and stock up again. Before we know it there are ten bottles of shampoo filling the cupboards and only one head on which to use them. A single bottle of shampoo can last for months, so that line of shampoo bottles equates to years of hair-washing capacity sitting there, ready to get scrubbing.

Our homes get clogged up with the 'good deals' and 'just in case' deals. Previous 'just in case' deals get smothered under newer purchases, soon forgotten, only to be pulled out in a spring clean or move years later and dumped. Don't get me wrong, I'm all for nice things, I love luxury and indulgence. However, when it comes to mindful spending, it's very much a quality over quantity situation that we're aiming for.

> 'Don't save anything for a special occasion, being alive is a special occasion.'
>
> Mary Engelbreit

How to Use Mindfully

Using mindfully means you only buy the item that you need when you need it and not a moment sooner. The rule, the only real rule for this habit to be a success, is to use up all the bottles, packets and samples that you have already before a new one can be bought. It's as simple as that.

To use mindfully, simply gather every piece of one type of product together. That product could be shower gels, face creams, body scrubs, exfoliators, lipsticks, nail varnishes, perfumes, blushers, you name it. The collection has to include samples, sachets, expensive versions, cheaper versions, every type and shape of that one product, without exception. Check every cupboard, press, car, room, handbag and box where bits might be hiding out. It is essential to take the time to do this. Gather them all into one place and line them up in a spot where they are easy to see and not forgotten about.

Bringing all the same type of item together allows you to see exactly how much you have of a product. It doesn't matter if it was a free sample or expensive splurge. It helps to lighten the pressure on your pocket and ensures you get value from the items on which your money is spent. This habit works well with minimalism, which we will get to in a later chapter.

Benefits of Use Mindfully

1. Saves Money

Using what you have already will mean that you don't have to buy that particular product for a while. Not purchasing replacements unless you are sure that you need it will give your wallet a break. It will also curb impulse spending on promotions and deals that you simply don't need. There will always be another great deal on somewhere when the time comes to purchase again.

2. Better for the Environment

Each product that's already in your home has been designed, formulated and tested to a high standard. It was then branded, packaged and shipped. After that, it was placed by a worker on a shelf ready for you to buy, which you gladly did. Then time and energy were spent bringing it to your home and storing it. Once there, it waits patiently to be loved and used by you.

The energy and resources expended on a product are significant. Many people have given their time and experience to get this product to you. You, in turn, have parted with your money for the privilege of buying it. The worst possible outcome there is that these products go to the landfill, unused. That would be a waste and a shame.

However, if you make a point of mindfully using whatever the item is, then the energy and resources have been worthwhile, and you get to benefit from it. If something must go to landfill, then at least send it after it has given all it can. You will feel better, and the world will be better for it.

3. Fresher Products

If you are one of the many people who save their good perfume for that rare occasion, then this one is for you. The best time to use a product is when it is new and in the prime of its freshness. Keeping things like perfumes or face creams for special occasions will do nothing more than give you an inferior experience. Many of these products contain natural ingredients that degrade over time. If left unused, they lose the unique properties that you bought them for in the first place.

Do it for yourself, get the best experience you can from the indulgent things in life and enjoy them when they are at their best.

4. Repurpose

Now and again a purchase comes in a particularly ornate box or interestingly shaped jar. When the container is empty, wash it out and repurpose it for something else. This way, you get to enjoy its loveliness for longer by giving it an extra lease of life as something new. Reusing things not only provides additional enjoyment; it's better for the environment and saves you money by not having to buy extra storage boxes.

5. Declutter

When it comes to things like beauty products, all those pots and jars can be hard to stack and store and they often end up as a messy jumbled heap in a drawer. They become a constant source of frustration because no matter how much you tidy, the area always looks jumbled. By taking the time to use each item and not replacing it until you have to, you are claiming back much-needed physical and mental space in your life.

6. Know What You Have, Love What You Have

A fun thing about using mindfully is that it allows you to figure out what you want from a product and not what you are told you want. Focus on the products that you have and figure out what's working for you and what's not. Spend time researching what is best for you and what you enjoy using.

Streamlining what you own will guide you towards buying things that you genuinely love and rule out the ones that you don't. The next purchase does not have to be the cheapest. Indulge a little more and spend on a better-quality product that you can relish and get benefits from, rather than several impulses that are just ok. One good jar of an €80 cream that you enjoy using and that feels excellent on your skin is superior to five or six cheaper pots for €15 each that don't make any difference, bring any sense of satisfaction and end up not being used.

7. Pamper Time

We are all busy, and time is rarely on our side. Setting yourself the goal of using mindfully and getting to the bottom of your beauty press guides you to take the time to pamper yourself. Make it a priority to use up all those fancy scrubs and jars that you keep meaning to get around to.

Set aside time each week for yourself and spoil yourself. It's to your benefit to take this time and enjoy what you have right at home. Waste not, want not, carve out pockets of time just for you. You are definitely worth that.

SUMMARY

Using mindfully will give your wallet and cabinets a much-needed break. It will help the environment, give you some much-needed time to yourself, maybe even accent your home with the repurposed things from time to time. Using mindfully will create more clarity around the products that you genuinely like and focus you on buying fewer but better products that are suited to your skin, age and personal preference.

This habit is not exclusive to beauty and makeup. It can be applied to food cupboards, office supplies and household products in any area, really. At the beginning of the No-Spend Year, I thought that I needed to install additional storage cupboards in my home. Now, thanks to this, I know all the products I own and enjoy every one of them with no extra storage required, saving even more money.

18

HABIT 6: MINDFUL MINIMALISM

Minimalism is about there being value and purpose in everything that you own. It is knowing that each item in your life is there for a reason, and that that particular reason makes your experience better. Minimalism is not owning a hundred objects or less, it is not downsizing to a studio apartment with one bowl that doubles as a cup and very little else. Minimalism has little to do with income and more to do with a state of mind. However, embracing minimalism can save so much money that your income will feel much more substantial.

Two big things differentiate mindful minimalism from everyday minimalism. Firstly, it is about you and your perception of what brings value to your world. It does not have to be the picture-perfect white walls and austere furniture. Mindful minimalism is ensuring that everything you own, everything you spend money on or receive, brings something to the table. Things do not have to match or be in perfect condition. It merely has to feel like home. However topsy turvy you want that home to be is entirely up to you.

The second differentiator of mindful minimalism is what happens to the items that are removed. Everything that does not bring value to you must be given every possible opportunity to have a second life. Whether it is through donating, passing on, selling or repurposing, what you do with these things is just as important as removing them from your personal space.

How to Become a Mindful Minimalist

Our world is bursting at the seams with innovative products and must-have gadgets. Our modern homes tend to be a reflection of this external wealth, resulting in stuff pouring into our lives day after day. Our homes get filled up with all sorts of unnecessary things. Many of these things come into our lives without us giving them too much thought. Each article is paid for, packed into a bag and brought home with eager delight. Soon the excitement of each purchase dwindles. Many of these items find their way into the dim recesses of a forgotten cupboard, never to be used to their full potential and often forgotten. Time, technology and trends move on, and soon the item is obsolete. Although some of these purchases are used, they are often of poor quality and don't last long. So we buy a mediocre replacement and store the old version away. The hope is that maybe one day it'll be fixed and used, but that rarely happens. Ultimately, in a fit of cleaning it is dumped into a skip, and more money is spent to haul it away. The cycle continues. When it comes to working your minimalist magic on your house and keeping it that way, the steps below are simple. Once the right mindset is adopted, keeping your home like this is straightforward, too.

Evaluate What You Have

Pick a room, any room in your home. Go through what is in that room and ask yourself why you bought it, or why it is there. Clothes, kitchen appliances, cushions, gadgets or cables, all these need to be evaluated. I picked cables there because when I did this in my home, I gathered all the disused wires around the house and by the time I had collected them all we had a massive tub of cables and wires that seemed to serve no purpose and yet cluttered up several presses, shelves and boxes. They were the culmination of years of technology flowing through our lives. The tablet may have died, but the cable was kept 'just in case'. Gather up all these 'just in case' things and prepare to give them a second life.

Keep What Works, Share the Rest

This doesn't mean simply throwing everything into the bin. Organise each type of item into piles – items for keeping, for selling, donating or repurposing. If something does not fall into any of these categories and has no hope of ever doing so then, and only then, consign it to the landfill. The easy option is to simply hire a skip and throw everything away. However, part of the mindful philosophy is to generate less waste. If there is a chance of an item having a second life, then it is better to strive for that. Once something hits the landfill, there is no going back.

Only one of the categories is to remain in the home, and that is the first one – and potentially a portion of the repurposing group. For the other items, there are so many creative ways to move them on. They may no longer serve a purpose in your life, but many things can benefit someone else. Where possible, don't be wasteful. This can take a little more time, but it is definitely worth it. The earth will thank you and you will feel better.

MAKE YOUR ROUTINE AS SIMPLE AS POSSIBLE

When it comes to decluttering a home and keeping it that way, it is essential to streamline routines as much as possible. When you clean your house, does it take you hours because you use so many different products? There's no need to have ten different cleaners sitting in your press. One or two great, multi-purpose cleaning products are more than enough. Products like an all-purpose homemade white vinegar and lemon cleaner, bicarbonate of soda and a good de-greaser should cover most cleaning needs. Whatever routine you have, try to find ways to simplify it so you can do things more efficiently. Generally speaking, as the number of items in your life is reduced, you'll naturally create a more straightforward routine for yourself, too. You might even gain some extra personal time.

THINK QUALITY OVER QUALITY

We have lots of wants all the time, which can be hard to fend off. However, most of us will have a particular weak spot, like kitchen gadgets, for example. There is an overwhelming array of kitchen helpers, such as avocado slicers, strawberry savers, herb scissors, garlic peelers – the list is endless. Most kitchen tasks can be handled with a handful of high-quality utensils and not 40 average ones.

While there's nothing wrong with having a wish list, it's essential to ask yourself whether these items will truly bring value to your life. Bear in mind that material items only tend to grant us happiness for a brief amount of time. When you feel tempted by the latest butter grater, pause and ask yourself if you would rather have that grater or a stress-free future.

PRACTICE GRATITUDE

It's essential to make every day count and acknowledge the good things. To live a mindful life, you have to be able to see all that you have. Creating a gratitude list helps remind us of the things to be grateful for. Interestingly, most of the gratitude that I have felt in my life revolves around people and experiences, rarely do material things make the cut. Practising gratitude regularly rewires the mind to prioritise what is truly important, and stuff becomes less important as a result.

THE BENEFITS OF MINDFUL MINIMALISM

The benefits of mindful minimalism are wide-reaching, not least in that it saves money. This habit saves you money in three ways: cash is generated from selling items that you no longer need but which still have value for someone else. Reducing the number of things that you own results in less minding, storage or maintenance, which lowers expenses. Thirdly, once you have given your home a good clear-out and find that you are happy with your space and see it as yours, there will be less of an inclination to fill it with unnecessary clutter again.

The result of this, over time, is to reduce or even eliminate the need to 'spring clean' your home. If everything in your life has a place and performs a function, then there is little chance that your home will fall prey to clutter cupboards and forgotten boxes again. The turnover of material things in your home will be significantly reduced, and you won't have to juggle items just to give them a once-over dusting.

Having fewer things means spending less time shopping and cleaning and more time for you. This time can be spent doing something that you've always thought about doing but never seemed to have the time to get around to. Maybe you like the idea of learning to play the guitar or piano but never got around to it because life was so busy. Perhaps art or cooking classes have been a dream of yours, but you thought that they were too expensive. The money freed up over time by mindful minimalism can be put towards developing who you are as a person and can help you to develop skills you've always wanted to have.

It's crucial to remember minimalism isn't just about stuff, it's about minimising in general. If you find that certain people in your life are energy vampires or take up more time than you have to give, mindful minimalism comes into play here, too. Clear out your schedule of events and people who do not make you happy and fill it with things that do. Embracing mindful minimalism is also better for the environment. Fewer things are bought, and the things that are purchased are kept for the long term. This means that, overall, fewer items end up in the landfill.

It gives you actual ownership of the space you live in and how you spend your time. Whether you are a homeowner or renting, making a place yours is essential for your mental health. Also, knowing where everything is will save days of your life looking for that lost set of keys.

SUMMARY

Minimalism is about assigning value and purpose to everything that is owned. It is knowing that each item is there for a reason, and that reason makes life better. Mindful minimalism takes things a step further, it does not follow a rigid structure. Instead, it focuses you purely on bringing your personality to your space instead of what you think you should have there. Mindful minimalism also insists that how the removed items are treated is just as important as how carefully we choose what remains. The landfill needs to be the last resort.

An exciting transformation takes place in a mind that embraces minimalism. By making the decision to only be surrounded by things that bring happiness and value, choices become much more manageable. Deprivation and loss disappear and are replaced by gratitude and freedom.

It also means, and I feel I can't repeat this enough, that there will be less cleaning, dusting, minding, servicing, insuring, storing, manoeuvring and organising. This gives you more time to do what you want with your life

Minimalism is a tool that can help you to find freedom. Freedom from fear, freedom from worry, freedom from overwhelm, freedom from guilt. Ultimately, freedom from the trappings of the consumer culture we've built our lives around. Real freedom.

19

HABIT 7: DIGITAL MINIMALISM

Digital minimalism is the online version of real-world minimalism. It takes each item, platform and media that you have in the virtual world and declutters it.

The online world has brought us so many benefits and has put anything we could ever desire at our fingertips. Gone are the days of the door-to-door encyclopaedia salesman – every drop of knowledge can be found at a moment's notice. Social media, online shopping, cryptocurrencies, digital photography and cloud computing have exploded into our lives in ways that we couldn't have imagined twenty years ago.

The internet, for the most part, has been a positive influence on our lives. Communication is faster and more reliable; anyone can contact a friend or family member at a moment's notice, free of charge. Team members can collaborate from anywhere. It has allowed us to become a global economy and has broken through the barrier that distance represented.

However, our online world has also become noisy, cluttered and often overwhelming. There are so many choices and options vying for our attention: online shopping, social media, apps, collaboration tools, learning tools and every form of entertainment imaginable. Every store has a sale, and every website has an event. Just like the real world, we can be hustled along by the rush of the tide, often losing hours of our life to the rabbit hole of the world wide web.

DIGITAL DETOXING DOES NOT WORK

The concept of the digital detox has been around for some time. Digital detoxing is where a person steps away from their online life for a while, usually a few days or weeks. Social media is set aside, and online activity is limited as much as possible. The idea behind a digital detox is to take a break from the urgency of the online world. When you are ready, or the detox time has passed, you come back to where you left off.

This does not work, because nothing has changed. The reason for the detox is still there. As soon as that phone is back in your hand, it is business as usual: the noise, urgency and stress return. It will only be a matter of time before another break is necessary. The online world should not be something that we should be running away from; you should embrace and use it as a tool to make life better, rather than allowing it to suck your energy.

DIGITAL MINIMALISM DOES WORK

Digital minimalism is different. Digital minimalism changes your digital world on a fundamental level. Like regular minimalism, various parts are assessed through the lens of need and value. Do I need it and/or does it bring value to my life?

If that app or platform does not make your life better in some way or does not have a definite purpose, then it must be removed and deleted. Whatever offerings are left are organised so they enhance your life in some way. The result is a quieter, less stressful digital life, one that is sustainable and that you don't need a break from. It is like turning down the volume of the online world. Forming the habit of engaging in digital minimalism will save time and a lot of money. Read on, and the reasons will become clear.

WHY PRACTICE DIGITAL MINIMALISM?

Digital minimalism is a long-term fix. It involves putting a system in place where things are organised around you and what you need from the online world. It cuts out the fuss, making the time you spend online calmer.

The reason why digital minimalism is a better option than digital detoxing is simply this: we are human. Sooner or later, humans want to be around other humans, in whatever form that takes, be it online or in the real world. We want to know what others are doing, saying or wearing. We want to be part of the action. This curiosity draws us back to old habits and the cycle starts all over again. Digital minimalism removes the need for sporadic detoxing because it deals with the core issues that cause us stress and cuts through the noise while keeping the part that works for you. It creates a perfect middle ground between the extremes of overwhelm and unplugging entirely.

> ## HOW TO KNOW IF DIGITAL MINIMALISM IS FOR YOU
>
> Do you:
>
> - Find yourself consistently browsing online even though there is nothing that you need?
> - Lose hours of your life to scrolling for no reason?
> - Spend more money online than you are comfortable with on things that you don't need?
> - Feel stressed when you open your inbox?
> - Find yourself always playing catch-up on several different social media platforms?
> - Get annoyed or distracted by notifications constantly pinging on your mobile?
> - Not recognise or remember half the numbers you have stored in your phone?
> - Not have photos on your phone that you haven't backed up in over a year, or maybe ever?
> - Have difficulty finding online documents when you need them, have no idea where they are stored in the cloud or on your phone or laptop?
> - Forget where most of the documents you need are or the name of the file they were stored in?
> - Have pages of apps on your phone, most of which are rarely used?
>
> If you answered yes to any of these, then you are in the right place.

HOW TO COMPLETE A DIGITAL MINIMALISM PROJECT

This sort of project can take time. The braver among you may intend to do this in one mammoth sitting. However, I recommend one task per day, as some tasks may take a little more time. Attempting to get an entire lifetime of online data under control in just a few hours is a huge task. Hence, I would like you to think of this as a work in progress and just like the tortoise in the fable, taking a slow and steady approach will make sure that you get there and do not run out of steam.

Some tasks will be completed quickly. Others will take a bit of time and thought. Once the habit is set up, it is easy to keep things in order after that. Keep with it until you are finished and you will be thankful that you did.

Be prepared to feel great once it is completed.

Be prepared to have a stress-free online life and even feel a little Zen.

Best of all, be prepared to have more money in your wallet.

Be prepared to never feel overwhelmed online again.

Step 1: Unsubscribe

Turn down the volume on your inbox with this step. Our inboxes have turned into a noisy market. We are bombarded with every sort of urgent message: Last-minute sale! Never-to-be-repeated deals! Unbelievable discounts! Limited time only! Not to be missed! The best discount ever!

My blood pressure went up just typing that. Everything in the world has an unbelievable discount on it – for a limited time only, of course. Although in my experience, the price cuts seem to be perpetual and the time limit never really runs out.

The Fix

To fix a noisy inbox, simply, go into the promotions tab in your inbox. Open the email that you want to stop, locate the unsubscribe button and click on it. It's usually found in tiny writing at the bottom of the email.

This will give you an excellent start to calming down your inbox. The rest can be unsubscribed from as new alerts land in your inbox. It will stop you from being tempted into spending money – money that you don't need to part with – while also giving you more quiet time to get productive work done that will actually bring in more money. This is a quick win.

Step 2: Clear Out Phone Contacts

There is so much history and emotional baggage tangled up in our phone contacts. Life moves forward and relationships change. Is it right sometimes to clear out the past and release the emotional energy trapped in those numbers? Old business contacts and company numbers are easy enough to delete. Most places have an online presence now. There is no need to have the number stored. If a number changes, it will automatically update on Google. Unfortunately, most phones don't do the same. Dealing with personal numbers can be a little more challenging, particularly if you are in any way emotional, which most of us are.

The Fix

To help decide if a contact should be kept or not, pull up the number and follow the reasoning below.

1. Life happens, and people drift: If a person hasn't been in contact in over a year and there's no urge to call them now to catch up, maybe it's time to accept that your lives have drifted apart, it happens. Delete it.
2. It isn't personal: the individual attached to the number has no idea that you're doing this. Their feelings won't be hurt. They don't get a notification. You may not have called them, but have they called you? Phone calls work both ways. Delete it.
3. It's not permanent: If a person desperately needs to be contacted again, it is generally a straightforward thing to do, thanks to social media and the internet. There is no need to keep a number just in case. Delete it.

Ridding your phone of names and numbers that are part of a past life or have no meaning to you anymore and moving forward with life is a cathartic thing to do. Funnel this newly released energy into building your future. Bye-bye boyfriend from 2004.

Step 3: Become Monogamous With Your Social Media

Count how many social media platforms you have a presence on. More than one? More than three? How many of these do you really enjoy and look forward to using? Do you spend time scrolling through notifications and alerts that don't mean anything, or are you constantly being distracted by notifications?

Social media can be a great source of information and enjoyment. However, it can also be a time vampire, sucking away hours a day of your life with little real benefit. Streamline your social media time to make sure you get the best out of it.

The Fix

Make your time online mean something:

1. Pick your favourite: Unless it is part of your job and you need to have more, choose the platform that you enjoy the most and feel is the best use of your social time.

2. Delete the rest. Hard to do, but why do you need to be part of so many? Chances are, the same people are on all of them. If not, there is always the option of just calling them.
3. Turn off notifications for your chosen social platform – this will prevent untimely distractions when you are trying to get work done.
4. Allocate a time: Pick a specific time during the day to revel in that platform. Look forward to it and enjoy it for all it has to offer. You will get more value out of it this way and won't be spreading yourself so thinly. It will allow you to focus on getting work done when it is supposed to be done.

A final note on social media: Even if you do delete your account, these companies don't hold grudges, you can always open one again in a matter of moments. You have lost nothing financially or emotionally by closing your account. You may even gain financially as you won't be tempted by the in-platform advertising.

Step 4: Documents and Files

How many documents do you have hidden in all corners of your inbox, laptop, cloud or, if you're old-school, external hard drive? If you are like most people, you will have no idea.

So what is the point in having all these essential documents and fond memories taking up your storage space if you have no idea where they are? If it isn't dealt with it becomes too overwhelming to tackle. It grows into an unwanted source of stress and costs money in storage, be it on a physical device or cloud subscription. If things aren't stored correctly and organised, precious memories and documents can be lost forever.

The Fix

1. Pick one place to store all your documents: cloud storage, a hard drive, whatever suits you best. Send as many records as you can find to that place.
2. Open new folders that are named correctly and efficiently so that you know straight away what's in there.
3. As you filter through the documents, place them in their specific folder. If need be, the folders can be subdivided, which will make storing future documents and finding existing ones super easy.
4. Copy to a backup to be doubly safe.

This will take a little while but is definitely worth it and will save you a lot of time in the long run. Note: Please do not delete any critical documents, particularly financial ones. Make sure that it is obsolete before you press that button.

Step 5: Online Photos and Media

We could all be better with backing up our photos and organising them. Some things are often underestimated when starting this section, such as the sheer volume of photos that we take. It may not feel like we take a lot, but they do accumulate over time. Many are duplicates. Why do we take 24 pictures of the same leaf from different angles and keep them all? I understand the need to take several group photos just to make sure we get one where everyone's eyes are open and looking at the camera. But when do we go back and delete the ones we don't need?

Photos tend to build up for years unchecked. I have a sneaking suspicion that they go feral after a while and start creating extra copies. Photos are actually time labyrinths in disguise. They suck you in with memories of all those great times. That first smile, the sunny holiday, all the things that make life worthwhile. The next thing you know hours have passed and you're only four photos in.

The Fix

This is, in my experience, the most significant task. I have found that the best course of action is as follows:

1. Get all your photos into one place.
2. Break the images down into years and then quarters or months.
3. Take a quarter at a time or a couple of months at a time and delete at least 50 per cent.
4. If there is an exceptional photo, put a copy of it in a specific folder on the desktop.
5. Keep going until the process is completed. This will organise your photos forever, and all you need to do from here on in is complete the same process once or twice a year with new photos.
6. This is the fun part. Open the folder with the especially precious photos that you found. Pick your top five favourites. Print them off and frame them for your home. That's what a picture was born to do. Put the good ones on show to enjoy the memories.

Step 6: The App Cull

Look through all the apps on your phone. Take note of any apps you do not use, do not remember ever using, or don't recognise. Yes, I'm betting there will be ones where you'll have no idea where they came from. These are for the chopping block. Particularly apps that have in-app purchases or ones that come with a monthly subscription fee (ensure that the subscription is cancelled for these before deleting). If you are not using it, why are you paying for it?

Just like social media, email subscriptions and most websites, there is the option to download and join app services again if you find that you are genuinely missing them.

SUMMARY

Taking the time to complete a digital minimalism project will reap dividends. Knowing that everything is organised and streamlined and knowing where to find a document brings great peace of mind.

The online world is a significant part of our lives. It is up to us to understand that, just like the real world, we need to structure it and ensure that the actions we take and the part we play in it go toward making our lives better, rather than adding stress.

Turning down the noise by deleting old numbers and unsubscribing from things will give you back mental energy. It will allow you to think more clearly about decisions and avoid online fatigue. The habit of practising digital minimalism prevents the need for digital detoxing and makes online time sustainable in the long term.

Part VI

MINDFUL MONEY IN PRACTICE: THE NO-SPEND YEAR

20

HOW THE NO-SPEND YEAR BEGAN

I had handed in my notice and was facing the unknown. There were things ahead of us that were outside my control, but what I could control, I had to make count. If I was going to single-handedly cut our income in half, then it was on me to ensure that what money was coming in worked as hard as it possibly could. 2019 was our year of change.

As with any good plan, there are rules: rules to abide by and to keep me on track. They needed to be robust and measurable, they needed to track progress, results, successes and failures. Above all, each rule had to cut costs as much as possible while still allowing us to live a good life.

I would keep a grocery budget and monitor essential bills to get the best value for money. Breakages, maintenance and kids outgrowing clothes had to be taken into consideration. That's life, it happens all the time. In these scenarios, purchases would be thought through with care before any money would be spent. New items could only come into the house if there was an urgent and specific need for them. To help me to keep spending under control, I decided to track all Spend Days and No-Spend Days each month, with a view to keeping Spend Days to a minimum.

I banned buying clothes, hair dye, going to the beauty salon, makeup, alcohol, eating out and buying takeaways for myself. I might have desperately wanted them, but I didn't need them. Embracing minimalism was a big part of the plan too. Truth be told, I'd been threatening this for the kid's rooms for years. Now I had a reason. Everything in our house would have its place. Anything that the kids had outgrown or didn't play with anymore would be re-homed. There was a pause on new gadgets, toys, clothes and any other impulsive purchases that tend to sneak into our cupboards. Anything else would be figured out as we went along.

THE FINAL MANIFESTO FOR THE GREAT NO-SPEND YEAR OF 2019:

This is the year that I live a full life without overspending. I want to remove the unnecessary spending and material things. I want to build a life of our design, not the life I think I should live. I want control over my time, to be with my children and to save for our future.

Tools to be used:

1. No-Spend Year
2. Minimalism

How it will be measured:

Grocery bill to be reduced by 50 per cent
Discretionary spending to be reduced by 40 per cent

How it will be achieved:

No Alcohol
Minimal eating out and takeaways
Meal planning
Spend tracking (No-Spend Days)
Comparison of all shopping bills
No new clothes
Personal spend reduction. No beauty/hair salon.
No dyeing hair
Selling or giving away any items that do not have a purpose
Reducing heating and electricity bills
Finding ways to have free family fun
Mindful spending
Sharing and swapping items with friends.
Low information diet – remove temptations of sales and special email offers by unsubscribing from as many services as possible

And any other means that I haven't thought of yet.
This is my promise to my family and myself for 2019.

This was the plan. These rules would be my guide. This was my choice, a choice that I voluntarily made. That said, I needed to put something in place to allow each member of the family to have autonomy. I didn't want to risk a coup three months in (or earlier) from my husband or kids, so the kids were given regular pocket money, which I cover in a later chapter.

As for my husband, for as long as we've been together, we've always combined finances. I'm not sure if it was ever a conscious decision or just naturally happened. I felt it would be unfair to ask him to give up everything alongside me. However, it would be equally unjust to the budget to have unplanned expenses leaving the account on an ad hoc basis. To keep things easy, each month an agreed amount was sent to a separate account just for him. That money was treated like any other bill, it had to be paid on time every month, no exceptions. This was his money to spend without account-ability. Whether he decided to eat out, buy clothes or fighter jets, the choice was his. It gave him freedom and independence to do the things that he wanted to do and left me to run with my little brainchild.

21

GETTING TO GRIPS WITH THE GROCERY BUDGET

When it came to the grocery budget, I tasked myself with halving what we had spent the previous year. In 2018 we had parted with €9,765.15 for food alone. An eye-watering amount for four people. I knew we threw out too much food unnecessarily. I also knew that there were more processed foods and short-cuts in our diet than I was comfortable with. These were the main factors that drove me to pare the grocery budget down to almost half of what it had been. These factors, as well as the knowledge that aside from our mortgage and transportation, food was the biggest single outgoing we had. Taming this expense was a high priority.

€100 per week or €5,200 for the year was the final amount decided on. This amount was for food, toiletries, cleaning products and household basics. It was an ambitious number, but if we succeeded, it could save us €5,000 – too high a figure not to try for. Could we sustain this regime for an entire year? Cut anything and you will save money, but cut too far and the fun gets knocked out.

The thought had crossed my mind to stock up on essentials before the project began. I could quickly get a year's supply of toilet roll, washing powder or other such staples and say nothing. A few well-chosen items would take the pressure off the budget. However, a combination of not wanting to deal with the guilt, mixed with being a terrible liar, pulled the plug on that idea almost straight away. I could not, in good conscience, stock up. It would defeat the spirit of the year. I was just going to have to do my best and muddle through.

It was more than just the money that I had to think about. This was to run for an entire 365 days; my children needed to thrive and not end up with scurvy or rickets. Saving money was the name of the game, but not at the risk of stunting their growth. The second significant consideration was to make sure that they continued to enjoy food. Both my husband and I are foodies. In the past, we have planned our holidays around good restaurants and food destinations. Taste and flavour are as crucial as health, and keeping a tasty and varied diet was as important to us as making savings.

Unfortunately, as much we loved good food, we were guilty of tending toward eating convenience food, having takeaways and eating out. Working long hours and feeling tired at the end of each day had led me to cut corners more often than I liked. Convenience food is expensive and I thoughtlessly spent the extra money to save time – but not anymore, not this year. I was rethinking my old habits. The time had come to change how I fed my family forever. I was on a mission to find the perfect balance between taste, health and finances.

Soon I was lamenting my decision – why hadn't I given myself more leeway? Cutting a growing family's food budget was a much bigger task than I had anticipated. There seemed to be so many things that needed buying each week. One minute I'd feel like I was in control, only to realise that we were out of milk, cereal or cat food, with little budget left. Other times I would go into the store with my list but then be distracted by promotions, shiny new products or tasty-looking snacks, inevitably returning home with impulse buys and other items that were definitely not on the list. It was a disaster. My mind just seemed to go on autopilot as soon as I stepped through those sliding doors.

I underestimated the power of habit and hadn't thought of food shopping in those terms. I was used to spending how I wanted and stocking up whenever the notion took me. Making several shopping runs per week, rarely bringing a list and wandering around aimlessly to see what caught my eye was the usual shopping mode.

The disorganisation showed in the meals, too, as I found that we would have a few tasty, healthy dinners during the week, but then the rest were made from a mishmash of what was left over in the house. I would almost have the makings of so many dishes but not the money in the budget to buy that one vital ingredient that would bring it together. I felt like a failure, and I was feeling the pressure.

A New Appreciation for Whiteboards

I knew the only way I was going to get the food budget under control was to build a system, but what would that system look like? I didn't know yet. What I did know was that it would start with me commandeering a small whiteboard from the kids. I propped it on the radiator in our kitchen. During the week, as essentials ran low, I would write them on the board. If anyone was running out of anything they needed, they were instructed to write it up themselves. If I came across a meal I wanted to cook, all the required ingredients went up there, too.

This whiteboard became my short-term memory and made the beginnings of a useful grocery list. Once the kids realised that they had a fighting chance of influencing the food budget, their handwriting improved noticeably. My daughter is now surprisingly good at copying my handwriting, and on more than one occasion I have come home with extra biscuits, strawberries and other sweet snacks because of it.

With the essentials recorded on the whiteboard, the next step was to check what we had in the fridge and freezer. Any opened jars or packets of food already present would be prioritised for the following week's meals. After this, I would check the supermarket apps to see what fruit and vegetables were on promotion that week, prioritising organic and Irish products where I could. I would mentally put together dinners, adding to the list what I needed to complete the meals as I went along. I would ask myself why was I buying something and what it was going to be used for. How likely was it to end up sitting on a shelf until it found its way to the bin, out of date or wilted beyond reclaim? With only €100 to work with, every saving made a difference. All those small choices, both positive and negative, would either make or break the food budget.

With the list sorted, it was time to focus on the shopping itself. Grocery shopping is a necessary part of running a home, but I didn't want it to take over, either, so, I tried to make it as straightforward as possible. I kept a box, shopping bags, trolley tokens and drawstring reusable fruit and vegetable bags stacked neatly in a spot in the kitchen. I gave myself a maximum of one hour to complete the whole shop. The time limit worked well to stop me languishing in aisles that I had no business being in (like convenience foods or home furnishings). This time limit ensured that I stayed focused and kept moving. It took some time to adjust. However, after several trips, I saw past the areas I would previously have been drawn to and focused on the task at hand: sticking to the shopping list.

Back home, I would pack everything away and write the meal plan onto the whiteboard. During the week, I would wipe the meals off as they were made and add the items that were needed for the next week's shopping. It felt good to finally be in control. We were eating better, and I was following the rules. The weekly expedition became less of a test of my willpower. I trained myself to get just what was on the list and not deviate from it, which historically had not been a strength of mine at all. It had in fact been my kryptonite. The shop was evolving from a fretful affair into a game, and a fun game at that.

A New Way of Eating

When it came to meals, meal planning was not my forte. However, I did have a few core dishes like curry, pizza, roasts and paella in my repertoire. By varying them with the fresh promotional produce each week, the meals were different enough to not feel tedious, while still making it easy for me to be consistent. Thankfully, this resulted in fewer complaints from my underage diners.

There were many unintentional changes in how we ate that year. One of the biggest surprises was that by meal planning this way, we were eating seasonally and our vegetable intake rose significantly. Another change was in the amount of meat that we ate. We rarely ate red meat, and when we did have it, it almost always came from the local butcher, ensuring that it was local and fresh.

For a while, supermarket chicken became our mainstay for protein. It was cheap and had a lower carbon footprint than the red meats. However, at one point I got the opportunity to buy organic free-range chicken from a local farmer. I remember baulking at the cost initially. I thought that the budget would never stretch that far. Nevertheless, we decided to give it a go and purchased a one-off chicken. The kids were sold immediately – they noticed the difference in texture and flavour straight away, as did I. That one chicken was all it took to convert us. The organic free-range birds were larger and lasted several meals. I bought one every week that I could and sometimes two, if money allowed. On the weeks where the organic chicken wasn't an option, I would get the best-quality free-range chicken available. Our meat supplier list was completed when a fishmonger at a local market was recommended to me and he quickly became our source of quality fish. I've always been fond of fish and, just like the chicken, the freshness and good quality were worth the extra cost.

22

AWAKENING TO FOOD WASTE

Getting a handle on what ended up in the bin was a crucial factor in controlling the food budget. I focused particularly on the organic waste bin as there was an €8.50 additional charge to the monthly refuse collection bill to get this bin collected, which to be fair is not a significant amount. However, it was when I had to think about our food that I started to see the organic bin as the serious money sucker that it was.

One evening I pulled the filled brown bin out to the kerb. It was a smaller one but was packed with months' worth of organic waste. I had to lever it on my hip to get it up on an angle so the wheels would roll. I was petrified that it would slip out of my hands and that the brown box would spew it stinking contents all over the driveway. On getting it to the edge of the path, ready for collection, it occurred to me. Each bin was filled with dozens of compostable plastic bags, which are much dearer than standard bags. Inside those compostable bags were kilos of food waste. Food waste made up of leftovers, spoiled veg, uneaten fruit, mouldy bread, out of date spices, peelings and other wasted food. Food that was meant to feed my family. So much was going into those bags each week. While heaving that bin around in the twilight I realised something had to change. The collection part was by far the cheapest aspect. It was the financial value of the food that filled it that made me take it seriously.

Everything in that bin had been edible at some stage. It had been grown, nurtured, harvested, cleaned, packed and shipped. From there, I handpicked it from the shelf in the store, paid for it, wrapped it, drove it home and stored it away until it was dumped into this very bin that I lugged out on that cold and miserable evening. Scared to death that if I dropped it, we would never have visitors again and be pariahs in our area because of the landfill stench. The effort, money and resources that had gone into filling up this bin … This innocuous €8.50 collection was, in reality, more like a several-hundred-euro bin collection. What could I do remedy this situation? How could I set this wastefulness to rights?

TACKLING FOOD WASTE

I set about thinking what I was going to do. First, I had to understand what I was putting into that bin. For the next week I watched and noted on a pad what was ending up in there. Its contents generally fell into one of these categories:

1. Peelings, ends and cuttings from fruits and vegetables.
2. Miscellaneous items like tea bags or coffee grounds.
3. Bones, leftovers and gone-off food.

Each of these needed to be dealt with individually. I wouldn't be able to eliminate all the waste, but I could, with a bit of work, make a sizeable reduction.

The volume of wilted and turned items that I was throwing away was simply too high. I hadn't thought that I was the worst offender when it came to food waste. However, when I caught myself tossing several rotten carrots, bananas and a mouldy orange into the compost one morning, I knew what I had to do.

I began checking the fruit bowl regularly and prioritised pieces that were close to turning. If I couldn't coax the kids to have them, I would wash, peel and slice them and put them in the freezer. Apple and pear work just as well in banana bread as bananas alone. Homemade cakes and treats made from the leftover fruit meant we would be less inclined to buy cakes or biscuits if we had sweet treats at home already. Other fruits would be kept for smoothies, crumbles, compote or desserts. Like the fruit, wilting veg got prepped for the freezer to be used in soups, stews or curries. Prioritising the prepped freezer food each week worked not only to reduce waste but meant that I had to buy fewer things when shopping.

THE FREEZER IN A NEW LIGHT

I learned to use our freezer differently, too. Previously, I just filled it randomly with various meats, vegetables and leftovers. I never really had a plan for anything in there. I began to look at the contents of my little chest freezer as money, real money locked away in a frozen account. Everything that was in there had cost money, and now, more money was being spent to keep it there in its frozen state in the humming freezer. I knew the deep freeze was primed for greater efficiency. What really intensified my urgency to get it under control was my friend. One day she lamented the amount of food she had lost when the electricity went while she was on holiday. Her chest freezer had been full, but it had all had to be dumped because nothing was salvageable by the time she got home. I was not putting my precious food budget at such risk.

I took inventory and set about using the contents up over several weeks. I focused on eating what we had there instead of buying more produce. If an item I needed was already in the freezer, it had priority. There was more food hidden away in there than I initially thought, good quality food just crying out to be eaten. This allowed us to not only free up space in the freezer but also took the pressure off the food budget for a while, giving me time to get a better handle on it. I went from having no clue what lay in the dark recesses of the freezer to knowing precisely what few items were stored there, when they had been bought and approximately when I was going to use them.

At this new, manageable level, I aimed for quick turnaround time on everything in there. I reasoned that living in a first-world country, surrounded by such a great selection of supermarkets and local shops, I could easily replace anything that was running out. My freezer was finally being used for what it was meant for, and that felt good.

EVALUATING OLD HABITS

With the efficiencies of the shopping list and freezer eliminated, I felt encouraged to find more. I looked carefully at what I was buying and why. There were things I would reach for out of habit, not thinking about how they fitted in with our diet. Fruit juice was the first big-ticket item on the chopping block. Good quality fruit juice is expensive. My kids love fruit, so I allowed them free rein over the fruit bowl. I also had a juicer, and quite a good one at that. I dusted it down and put it to work. Between the homemade juice and fruit bowl freedom, they got ample vitamin C and other fruit-derived nutrients in their diets, which more than compensated for the lack of store-bought juice.

Yoghurts, in general, got their marching orders too. My kids love milk, butter and cheese and would happily eat their body weight in dairy. Yoghurts were superfluous for us, as they're high in sugar and have too much packaging. So off the list they went. I ensured that there were homemade cookies or flapjacks for them if they wanted a sweet snack. I did keep yoghurt for cooking and desserts, but that was it. I ensured that there were homemade cookies or flapjacks for the kids if they wanted a sweet snack. Bottled and sparkling water also disappeared. I had a soda stream maker and water filter at home already, so why I was buying those items in the first place, I will never know. Other things like kitchen roll and wet wipes got their marching orders too and were replaced by homemade versions.

The next big food waste area to tackle were the cuttings and peelings from fruit and vegetables. This was probably the single biggest contributor to organic waste for us. Initially, these stumped me, purely because I had always seen this waste as OK. But now I had to rethink my old habits. After some research, I found out that so much of what I was throwing out was in reality entirely edible and often nutritious.

Simple things like the stems of broccoli, or cauliflower leaves, can be roasted along with the rest. Also, many seeds like pumpkin and squash seeds can be toasted and made into a great savoury snack. Orange and lemon skins can be dried and used as a tea or to make a tasty oil dressing. One of the biggest hits in our house when it came to reclaiming that food waste was potato peelings. Usually, I would have just thrown those out, but I learned they could be rinsed and stored in the fridge in salted water. When a tasty snack was called for they were patted dry and fried up like crisps. A whole new world of food opened up to us.

We invested in a compost bin for the garden. I had toyed with the idea of making a homemade one, but my husband firmly talked me out of it, citing the fact that my handy skills were not handy at all and that I regularly ended up calling a professional in to fix the mess I made. So following that word of caution, I found one at a reasonable price and proudly placed it at the end of the garden.

All these initiatives and many others worked together to significantly reduce the amount of food waste we created. I have a new appreciation for the zero-waste movement and I get a great sense of satisfaction from making the most of the food we eat. Using the food that we buy more efficiently has allowed us to raise the quality of that food overall. This year I purchased more organic, fair trade, free-range and ethically sourced food than ever before with the smallest budget that we have ever had. That is something that feels very good indeed.

23

THE LUNCH BOX DEBATE

It wasn't just me that had to adjust to the food budget. The rest of the family had to adapt in their own ways, too. It became evident to them that things were changing when I interfered with the status quo of their school snacks. I wanted to see how I could improve their lunches while keeping the budget in check. Historically, their lunches weren't lousy per se, there was always at least one fruit and veg, a sandwich or wrap and a small treat. The treat was usually popcorn, a cookie or, if I caved in the supermarket, cheese dippers, Lunchables or one of those yoghurts with the fruit in the corner. Unfortunately for my offspring, the latter convenience foods were not on this year's list. Processed options were outside the budget, so they had to make do with homemade cookies instead. It felt like a good compromise to me, but sadly they didn't share my view.

They were missing the street cred of branded snacks in their lunch boxes. 'All the other kids have this in their lunch box or that in their lunch box, why don't we?' came the whines. I tried different tactics to get them to come around to my way of thinking. I even tried to talk with them about the positive health benefits. I described in great detail how they would grow as people and see the world from a different viewpoint. All they had to do was embrace who they were and understand that what was in their lunch boxes didn't define who they were as people. I explained how they would know who their friends were because real friends wouldn't judge them for the contents of their lunchboxes or the number of new toys they received. A real friend would love them for who they were. I finished with a flourish, leaving my meaningful message to hang in the air for effect. After a moment's silence, they turned to each other and erupted in fits of laughter. It's a long time since they've laughed that hard.

Once they had composed themselves, I endeavoured to make a truce. We discussed what might work. After many disagreements, we settled on Tuc crackers. I would give them two crackers each in their lunch box along with their current offering. This compromise seemed agreeable and it was resolved – or so I thought.

It turned out that it was not settled. When they arrived home after the first day of the new concession, they were not impressed. 'Why didn't you put the *real* Tuc in my lunch box?' was the greeting as two cooler bags were slapped on the table. Two sets of eyes watched me, waiting for a response. 'I did,' came my reply. It turned out that I had not. The ones that I had given them didn't have the brand name mechanically embossed on the crackers themselves. So they could not be real, hence they obviously tasted awful. I was told categorically that I had ruined yet another lunching experience and if I was not careful, I was on track to ruin their lives completely. This year was the worst, they claimed, and we had to stop being poor.

Now, just to be clear, to me a cracker is a cracker, whether it is branded or generic (sorry, Tuc) so I picked up the cheaper pack when I was shopping. However, according to my knowledgeable children, my assumption was wholly inaccurate, and I had to fix the situation immediately. I knew that it would be several days before I was due to go shopping again and I was not making a trip specifically for one packet of crackers that I did not want them eating in the first place. So, to attempt to salvage the situation again, I offered to emboss the biscuits myself with bespoke lettering using a compass. They didn't go for it and the offer was flatly refused. I wasn't ready to give up yet, so I asked them to hold off with the criticism and see how they got on with the rest of the packet. I think I was hoping that they would just get used to it and accept my shoddy parenting and generic biscuits.

Again, no such luck. That same week, they began to disappear to my neighbour's house after school. I didn't mind at first, as their friends lived there. I assumed that they were playing. That was until I realised the timings of their absences were quite suspicious. They would disappear just before dinner and never for more than 15-20 minutes. It struck me as odd, as time-keeping was not a strength either of my kids possessed. So I spoke with my neighbour to see if she could shed some light on the matter. She told me that each afternoon they would call over and inquire after her Tuc crackers. She's a kind woman and knew this was her cue to offer them. They'd demolish their ration and return home, delighted with their ingenuity.

The sneaky little things never said a word to me, though they had recently compared my parenting techniques with hers and had concluded that my friend's parenting skills far surpassed mine. They even felt the need to remark on how great it would be if they could swap us over and have her as their new mom. To avoid the risk of dealing with an emancipation lawsuit, I thought that, for this one at least, I had better concede and put the real Tuc back on the shopping list. I would have to find other places to curb spending.

FORAY INTO OTHER CUISINES

The Tuc incident wasn't the only mistake that I made with the food budget. At one stage I got restless and took a notion to change things up and try another cuisine. I've always liked stir-fries and Thai and Chinese food, but my husband doesn't share my enthusiasm, he leans more toward Indian, Italian and Spanish food (which I thankfully also enjoy). A friend of mine was clearing out her cookbook collection and gave me one on Chinese cooking. I read through it and found several tasty-sounding recipes to try out. Even though we didn't have a wok, I had images in my head of sautéing vegetables and skilfully tossing colourful noodle dishes into the air, deftly catching it all back into the pan. Easy-peasy, I thought.

I invested a chunk of our food budget into gathering the necessary basic sauces, oils and condiments that were required to make an authentic version of these dishes. A couple of meals in I realised what a mistake this had been. Not only does it take a lot more skill than I thought to toss sautéed vegetables in the air as they do on TV, but there's a bit of flair required to bring proper flavour to these dishes, something that simply eluded me. I thought that it was just me and that maybe I didn't like Chinese food as much as I thought. I resolved to stay quiet about it, because if everyone else was enjoying it, there was no reason for me not to continue cooking it. After all, the cupboard was now overflowing with sauces, vinegars, pastes and oils explicitly purchased for this purpose. I was not allowing those to go to waste if I could help it.

Unfortunately, the lacklustre meals did not go unnoticed. Soon, every dinner was accompanied by unrelenting critical reviews of my efforts. I urged them to have an open mind and to keep trying – it was a different style of cooking, after all. Eventually, I gave up. It wasn't worth the learning curve or the cacophony of abuse. I still have a cupboard that would make any Cantonese person proud, and I'm promising myself that I'll make another go if it, maybe. For the moment, at least, I believe that Asian food is best left to the professionals.

DISAPPOINTED CATS

It wasn't just the kids who were continually disappointed this year. The cats had their fair share of letdowns, too. They were just coming out of the kitten stage and had been on pouches of food, which they relished. Unfortunately for the cats, I realised that the sachets were not recyclable and were generating a lot of packaging waste. So I moved them onto tinned food, which was an improvement, but I felt like there was just as much packaging with tins. There had to be better options. After some research, I found that cats are obligate carnivores and unlike dogs need a high-protein diet to stay healthy in the long term. This led me to try good quality dry food. I was proud of myself for thinking of the long-term health of our spoiled pets by squeezing this pricey option into the budget.

Things went well for a while. Their coats got fluffier and soon they looked like they had come out of the tumble dryer. That was until the morning the male cat came in and left red puddles all over the kitchen floor. He was not well, and I knew a trip to the vet was in order. As it turned out, neutered male cats are prone to this sort of infection and chances were that it was related to his food. So I had to change it up again. Unsurprisingly, my best option for this fussy, lactose-intolerant, allergy-prone and generally disdainful creature was to feed him even more expensive food. He was also declared overweight, so he had to go on a diet. The food cutbacks resulted in him hunting me around the house for the next few weeks, bawling miserably, wondering when his next meal would be. If I didn't send him to the animal shelter then, I never will.

NOT ALL FOOD FAILED

Even though some of the food experiences did not go as well as hoped, some did. Organising the food cupboards was a more successful one. Packages, jars, bottles and boxes were all checked for use by dates and restacked accordingly. Out of date items were removed and disposed of, while items bought for one-off recipes or close to their use-by date were placed in a box on the countertop. The heap of odd products sat before me like a monument to poor shopping choices. Each week as I planned the meals for the coming days, the box was consulted. The game was to create a family meal incorporating as many things from the box as possible. This worked to reduce waste and to free up some badly needed storage space. The game provided several surprise discoveries. Smoked paprika, which had been lingering in the spice cupboard unused for ages, gives dishes a rich, smoky flavour. It even works well sprinkled over chips, elevating them to the next level of tasty. By the same token, I've exiled both Vegemite and Marmite from our house. After many efforts to make them work in dishes, they just don't seem to want to.

24

SCRAP PLANTS

One afternoon, I was attempting to get the kids eating guacamole. It wasn't one of my greatest successes by any margin. After many wrinkled noses and claims that I was trying to murder then, I appeased the pair by augmenting the recipe so much that it hardly looked or tasted like guacamole anymore. My only consolation was that it was still a sort of green colour, even if it had lost all its nutritional value. In the end, I wondered if it was little more than an exercise in tortilla consumption.

It was my son in his favourite thinking chair that triggered the chain of events that followed. He picked up the discarded avocado stones and was busily rubbing them on the tablecloth, trying to get the last of the flesh off the seed. Briefly, I wondered what life would be like if his efforts involved stain removal instead of stain generation. Leaving my fanciful thinking behind, I watched until he had polished it to a satisfactory level. Then, holding out the brown, teardrop-shaped stone, he asked in a serious tone, 'What are these, Mom?' I explained that they were the seeds of the avocado plant, and it was from these that the avocado tree grew. His eyes lit up, the cogs in his head could be heard whirring to life. The thought of having a tree growing in his room was irresistible. 'Mom, can I grow one?'. I smiled and responded, 'Sure, just as soon as you've cleared that plate.'

We washed out old jam jars and rooted for the wooden toothpicks. After a bit of fuss, we stood back to admire the row of three pierced, wobbly avocado stones perched on top of their new jam jar homes. After admiring their handiwork, the children carried the seedlings off to their new homes, one for each bedroom and one for the kitchen window. A resounding, 'Yes,

Mom, we'll take care of them', echoed down the hall as they whisked their new projects away. Over the next few weeks one of the three stones – my daughter's – sprouted roots and eventually a shoot. We transferred it to potting soil and placed it on her window, where it still sits today. As more avocado stones came into the house through the grocery shopping, we planted them. Soon we had several impressive avocado plants adorning the windowsills of our home. They are such a pretty plant, with its tall thin stalk and umbrella-style leaves, unpretentious and elegant. It is the perfect plant for the minimalist in your life. The kids took great pride in showing them off to anyone who visited.

After the success with the avocado plants, the kids set their sights on the compost bin for more gardening projects. We had many failures. However, we had successes, too. Five organic lemon seed pips have grown into five shiny green lemon saplings. Ginger root, carrot tops, garlic, and celery stumps also grew well. We tried our hand at garlic bulbs, onion roots, pepper seeds and mango with varying degrees of success. The children took satisfaction in knowing that they were part of the process, and I took equal pleasure in growing something from what I would generally have considered waste. From that point on we were bitten by the re-use bug and there was no going back.

There's a small herb patch in the back garden; it wasn't very tidy or organised. Nevertheless, it became the perfect nursery for the seeds and bulbs rescued from the bin. We planted several potted herbs bought for cooking that were reaching the end of their culinary life. Many of these, once repotted, regenerated quite happily. By the end of the year, we had abundant oregano, rosemary, coriander, thyme and parsley. The parsley did particularly well, thriving in our boggy old soil.

WILD FOOD ADVENTURES

One afternoon my kids rocked into the kitchen, panting, with bags full of apples from one of our neighbours. He had let them pick 'a few', but to judge by their rosy faces and heavily laden backs, their version of 'a few' was bigger than most. In their humble yet noisy opinion, they were the best hunter gathers to ever roam the planet. The haul was dumped unceremoniously at my feet as they proceeded to bounce around the kitchen, listing out all the things that they were going to make and bake. My son, who has a particular love of apples, had ideas of living off them for the whole winter. He was more than a little crestfallen when I told him that a diet made up solely of apples would not suffice for a growing boy.

We set to work making apple juice, apple jelly, apple puree and dried apple slices. Up until that point, they had only ever known bought versions of these things. Never having thought about how apple juice got into the carton or how jam was made, it was a bit of a revelation to them. I felt guilty for never having taught them; I had the skills from my childhood but in recent years I had left those skills behind. It was time to dust them down and pass some on to the kids. They embraced the idea with great enthusiasm. Enjoying the novel processes and seeing how things were made was new and exciting for them – although I do believe that part of the excitement could be directly linked to the newfound awareness that a large amount of sugar would be involved. An impressive store of apple-based products was made that lasted for months.

Spurred on by a cupboard stocked with apple products, the kids later headed out on raspberry, blackberry, elderberry and hazelnut picking expeditions. I could barely keep up with them. Their keenness for collecting was infectious, although just like the apples, I believe a large proportion of the enthusiasm was because they paid themselves handsomely in produce, returning home from their adventures with full bellies and half-full bowls.

It was around this time that they had the idea of collecting wildflower seeds. We gathered wild seeds while on walks and stored them in an old flour bag. The plan was to create a small space in our garden to grow wildflowers to encourage bees. Each time we went out picking berries, we would collect more seeds. Over time we built up a nice little stash, for flowers of all sorts of fantastic colours and shapes. I had never noticed the variety of beautiful wildflowers we have in this country. Soon we had much more than we needed for our little garden patch, so we came up with the plan to sow them around our local area. The bees wouldn't mind where they went for their flower nectar and the following summer the ditches near us were awash with colour and teeming with life.

The excitement for the picking and foraging stuck with the kids, giving us many fun, No-Spend Days out. We would cycle to some of the local woods and hidden hedgerows in search of berries or take short drives to ones further afield. It was a fun way to spend an afternoon; we'd pack a small picnic, bring our buckets and go hunting. Being out in the fresh air on those afternoons with only the twittering of birds and the chatter of my offspring were some of the loveliest memories I have of the year.

25

CLEANING SUPPLIES

Household and cleaning products received a total overhaul that year. Most single-use disposable things like cleaning wipes became a thing of the past. I did miss the convenience, but they were an extra expense that would be heading straight to landfill after only a few minutes of use. Old towels and t-shirts were used as cleaning rags instead. They were cut into a usable size and stored with the other cleaning products so they could be easily used when needed.

Many of my old store-bought cleaning products were replaced with white vinegar and bicarbonate of soda. A trip to the local cash and carry stocked me with litres of vinegar and drums of baking soda for only a few euro. Bicarbonate of soda is an excellent mild abrasive and cleaner for stubborn stains on pans. It is also useful when it comes to deodorising carpets and beds. Simply sprinkle on mattresses, soft furnishings or carpets, leave for 20 minutes to work its magic and then hoover away. Adding a few drops of essential oil to the powder will leave the area smelling wonderful.

White vinegar proved to be a great all-rounder, too. It's eco-friendly and doesn't contain extra chemicals. I discovered that if lemon rinds are soaked in a jar of vinegar for a couple of weeks, the scent and oils mellow out the astringent smell. If the peels are then decanted and mixed equal parts vinegar and water, the result is a lovely natural lemon-scented surface cleaner. Be sure to patch test any new surface when trying for the first time.

Many other home cleaning products got the homemade makeover: room spray, carpet freshener, surface cleaner, toilet cleaner, floor cleaner, window cleaner, even detangler for my girl's hair. A few essential items did stay on the list, like washing powder and degreaser – those I did not manage to master. However, for the most part, cleaning products can now be found in a tiny little storage space under my sink. My home is clean, and I feel better not having as many chemicals in the house. The cost of cleaning the home now is practically nothing.

I found that if white vinegar was applied neat, it was a good substitute for chemical weed killer. It knocked back weeds to a sustainable level without harming flora and fauna unnecessarily. It was a big factor in allowing my gardening to go eco-friendly. It feels good to hear the buzzing of all those busy little insects in the summer and was something that I hadn't realised I had missed in my garden. The oregano and other herbs that we had planted were practically vibrating with the humming. I would often bring a cup of coffee down and sit in the garden and watch them bustling from flower to flower, it was such a pleasure.

A FINAL NOTE ON FOOD

As the year progressed, managing the food budget became easier. Not every week was perfect, but things seemed to be going in the right direction. One thing had weighed on my mind from the outset though, and that was Christmas. December stood out to me as potentially being a budgetary problem. Christmas is a time for being generous and for me, food is one of my most significant ways of showing that. To ensure that there were enough funds for that time of year, I carried forward any under-spends from my weekly budget to be used over the Christmas period. This would give me the leeway to spend more over Christmas while sticking to the budget overall.

Keeping to the food budget was work; however, I feel that it was time well spent. It was time well spent for many reasons. Not only was there an improvement in our diets with its potential health benefits, there was also reduced waste and we had less of an environmental impact, in addition to the significant financial impact it had on us. We ended up spending only half the amount that we would have spent on food in previous years, and have never eaten so well. The refuse charges also dropped, as we produced notably less waste and packaging that year.

26

SHAKING UP THE VANITY

The evening the beauty rules went into the manifesto was a difficult one, particularly at the start of the No-Spend Year. I was sitting by the fire sipping a glass of wine, the wine I had not committed to giving up just yet. I reasoned that not dyeing my hair, buying makeup or going to the salon would be great money-savers and easy to do, surely. The more I cut my outgoings, the less pressure on our finances, the easier it would be to take this time with the kids. A thing that was worth infinitely more than my vanity. My rational mind nodded sagely, while the conceited part of me was unconvinced.

The first couple of months were the worst. As the blonde grew out, the unwelcome straight line separating coloured from natural worked its way down my crown. This I could handle, even embrace as edgy, but this regrowth was not my usual sandy blonde. This regrowth was generously dappled with white – there was no hiding my age now. This was going to take some getting used to.

As with my hair, for the first time in decades I had to contend with the natural state of my lashes and brows. My colouring is fair, which from a distance gives me a pallid, tired appearance. I meted out the limited makeup supply carefully, not sure if I could get through the next few months, let alone a year. Ironically, it was because of this fear that I began to wear less and less makeup. Often none, thus exacerbating my insecurities.

When shopping, running errands or visiting friends, I felt like the world was judging me. My inner voice would insist on telling me what a disgrace I was, and how I was letting myself go. I felt unkempt and older than my years. I've never considered myself pretty, but I try to be well turned out and take pride in my appearance. I saw it as a sign of respect for myself and my respect for others, plus I love the ritual of applying skincare and makeup. I was missing them badly.

One morning I found myself standing in front of the mirror, looking at the tired face staring back at me. The dull hair and pale skin, lashes and brows were all that I could focus on. I felt I was becoming invisible, old and invisible. Peeling back the layers of hair and makeup revealed the real me for the first time in my adult life. It was scary. The insecurity caused by being outside my comfort zone was creeping in. This time I didn't have the consolation of knowing that there was a salon appointment or makeup counter trip on the horizon. This washed-out version of me was hard to handle. The world was seeing me for who I was, a basic run-of-the-mill ageing mouse. I thought I was above that sort of weakness. It turned out I wasn't.

HONESTY HURTS

That same morning I walked into the kitchen to find the children in deep conversation. As I closed the door behind me, two pairs of meerkat eyes shot glances in my direction and silence filled the room. Their previous chat has been about me, that much I knew. I braced myself for what was coming. Between mouthfuls of cereal, my son asked, 'Mom, why are you so old?' His sister piped up, 'Yeah Mom, why do you look so old?' As a rule, I encourage my kids to ask questions and be honest. However, there are times when I wish they weren't so forthright. This was one of those times – I wasn't robust enough at that moment to brush their innocent questions off. I kept my mouth shut, trying not to get emotional.

I steadied myself and forced a smile. 'What makes you ask that, honey?'

'Well', my son answered, 'you have grey hair, and old people have grey hair, so I think you must be a million'. My daughter burst out laughing, 'Don't be silly, Mom is not a million, people aren't a million,' she continued, 'but she does have grey hair, and Nannie has red hair; therefore, she must be older than Nannie. So I think that she must be a hundred.' She beamed, proud of her astute deduction.

Taking mental notes to limit their access to the TV and revisit some stereotypes, I informed my dears that I was not in fact a hundred years old. It so happened that grey hair was perfectly acceptable; there was nothing wrong with it. This was how I looked. I was happy with my comeback and thought that would put an end to the discussion. However, it was my daughter who got the last word in. She concluded, 'So you are not old, you just want to look old'. This made some sort of satisfactory sense to her, and I was lost for words. She went back to the pressing task of eating her cereal.

I left the kitchen and stood in front of the bathroom mirror again. With my children's words ringing in my ears and tears stinging my eyes, I drank in the person staring back at me. This was not who I was, this was not the path I wanted to take. I wanted a better life; I didn't want to give up on myself. There had to be a balance. I was better than this. For my children, I had to be better than this. Pursing my lips, I made eye contact with the defeatist creature reflected in the mirror. I took a few deep breaths and gathered myself. I had designed this year, I had made these life choices, and it was up to me to make it work. It was my responsibility to step up and get my head straight.

Reality had to be faced, this was not a time for self-pity. My skin and hair did not grow dull because I had stepped back from my career, nor was it because I cut our income in half. My skin and hair had changed because I had stopped taking care of it as I had done before. I was not giving it the time it needed, and the thoughtfulness required to keep it healthy. That was nothing to do with income, that was directly linked to my mood and how I felt about myself. The negative internal monologue had to go, now was a time for action.

Throwing money at my problem was not an option anymore. It was up to me to resolve this dilemma. I had to use what was available to me. I researched homemade skincare, soaps, moisturisers, cleansers, scrubs and masks, picking up a whole new raft of tips and advice on handmade products. I researched face masks and hair masks to nourish and bring a bit of lustre back. Oil, oatmeal, spices and fruits became staples in my new skincare regime. Brown sugar mixed with oil and cinnamon made a moisturising shower scrub. Coconut oil, it turns out, is a great facial cleanser. Honey with ground almonds is a nourishing face mask. A whole new world of skincare opened to me, and I embraced it with enthusiasm.

Exercising also entered my routine, along with a renewed commitment to healthier eating. The exercise wasn't super strenuous, but it worked well to get me out of my head and outside more. If I felt low, tired or was doubting myself, I would throw on my runners and get outside, which generally gave me the lift that I craved. The double win was, if I was out walking or running I wasn't inside being tempted by online shopping. My diet was ok – it was much better, thanks to the new food budget. The newly increased fruit and vegetable intake improved my skin from the inside over time.

MAKING IT WORK

I endeavoured to mindfully use up all my existing makeup, beauty products and hair treatments and was determined to use everything in my current arsenal. Leaving jars and pots sitting in the press for a special occasion simply wasn't an option anymore. Ironically, the very fact that I wasn't utilising them was just like not having them at all. There was no better time than now, when my skin needed it the most. I started applying all the little bottles and pots of magic potions and samples that were hiding in the back of my cupboard. It amazed me how many products lurked in there, most of which I'd forgotten I even owned. All the little samples and jars that I just collected for no real purpose were now lined up, ready to be used.

The game of using up every bit of a product overflowed onto my Instagram account. A group of us got together and posted photos of all our empties. The challenge, which we playfully dubbed the 'Use up challenge', was not to buy any new products until the existing ones were used up. It became an infectious habit that continued well past the month of August, when we had started it. There was satisfaction in making full use of a product and getting the best value from it. This was a better outcome than being lost in the back of a cupboard, only to be binned in some frantic spring clean years from now.

I changed up my makeup regime and went for the less is more approach. I watched YouTube videos on how to get what I had to last longer, and I learned to substitute one product for another. My eyebrow pencil ran out early in the game, and I learned that matte eye shadow worked just as well, perhaps a little better, in giving the brows some shape. Foundation could be blended with moisturiser to give tinted coverage and to double how long it lasted. Lipsticks became blushers, and a drop of makeup-remover brings a mascara nicely back to life. I practised with eye shadow colours that I would have previously ignored in my palettes, with the odd pleasant result. For all my initial fretting about makeup, what I had lasted me for the entire year. All thanks to a bit of innovative thinking and a lot of advice from some sharp cosmetics-savvy friends.

When it came to hair products, after the expensive shampoos were gone I tried the children's one. It was of the sensitive, all-natural sort, and it worked wonderfully. Not chemically treating my hair every few weeks negated the for need shelves full of expensive, specialised shampoos. This was a bit of revelation after years of buying overpriced hair products that promised magical results. In the end, it took a simple, natural, straightforward approach to give me the best, fastest growing and healthiest-looking hair I have ever had. Having such a simple regime freed up time and money that I never had before.

I came across several online accounts from women who had given up dyeing their hair and embraced their natural silver locks. They all, without exception, looked fantastic. None of them seemed, tired, worn out or invisible. They all looked like regal and confident women. I don't know if I'll ever be something to be reckoned with like they are, but I wasn't going to let my sniping ego wear me down any longer. I learned to adjust to my white streaks. When I wear my hair down the white shows up as two great stripes of highlights at the front, and tying it up reveals a whole swatch of dappled grey at the sides. The kids thoughtfully pointed out to me that I look like a calico guinea pig, or sometimes Cruella De Vil, depending on what form they are in. I'm ok with that – at least I'm not a million years old anymore.

WHAT REALLY MATTERS

I don't feel so vulnerable about my hair now. I'm even coming to terms with the persistent cowlicks. I've learned a big lesson in the process. The lesson is, vanity is first and foremost in my mind. If I feel below par, I interact with the world in a below-par way. That translates to the things I do, the words I say and the way I react to others around me. If I own who I am and what I look like, that translates too. Let's be frank here, I am not interesting enough to waste your time on judging.

At the beginning of the year, I had a moment where I looked at things the wrong way. I don't judge my friends for not wearing makeup and neither did I think anything of them going to the salon. These things don't even rate when it comes to the stuff that matters. The things that I love and admire in my friends were never superficial. It was always something more profound. It was their confidence, quirkiness, odd sense of humour, or owning who they were. I was never their looks; it was their natural charm and passion for life. That is the friendship I seek, and that is what I want my friends to look for in me. It was I who was judging myself, and I was the harshest judge of them all. I realised that it didn't matter what colour or texture my hair was as long as I took care of it and wore it with pride, just like those silver-haired women did, just like anyone should.

I can't say that I was perfect and impervious from there on in, but what I do know is that it is ok not to be perfect all the time. I don't want to compete with or keep up with anyone anymore. I want to own who I am, and that is a very freeing experience.

27

A NEW APPRECIATION FOR APPAREL

During the summer, my last pair of fitted blue jeans split. I was gutted. I'd practically lived in them, and they were my favourite. My daughter found this hilarious. She made it her mission to spread the word of my misfortune. Word spread quickly, and one of my neighbours sent down a pair that didn't fit her anymore. It felt strange to accept them, but I knew from my pathetic sewing skills that my options were thin on the ground. Nervously, I tried them on. I pulled them up and fastened the button and stood for a moment. I gave a wiggle and a lunge. They were the best fitting jeans that I had worn in my entire life. They were soft and comfortable and my legs were in jean heaven. I danced around the room in delight. These were the perfect solution to my problem; I could have hugged my friend there and then. That one thoughtful gesture has made a loyal customer of this brand of jeans for life.

The jean incident made me understand what it felt like to receive something that was needed. We had given away many of our possessions earlier in the year to friends and through donations. It had felt good to give. However, this was the first time I had received something for myself, something that I genuinely needed. It felt good.

Clad in my new jeans a sense of optimism flowed through me and I decided to take inventory of what remained of my clothes. I pulled the wardrobe door open and began to rummage. Many items were holding up well, others were becoming worn and showing signs of age. Frayed cuffs and splitting collars were appearing. One garment was coming undone at the seam, while another needed a button.

There were a few core pieces that I practically lived in – my comfy, everyday clothes. These were the fraying items, the things I wore regularly, too regularly. Feeling the aged material in my hands recalled fond memories made while wearing them. A surge of respect for these clothes that had served me so well welled up. They owed me absolutely nothing. From the pressed designer cotton shirt to the lowly winter vest, these loyal things had done their jobs admirably.

I wasn't used to having so many items in my closet that were genuinely worn through. Usually, clothes were replaced whether I needed them or not. I was so guilty of opening my wardrobe to find it brimming with clothes and then declaring there was nothing to wear.

GOODBYE FAST FASHION

In January, minimalism first worked its magic on me. It had been easy to make the decision to move the 'on trend' clothes out of my life. Any fast fashion I owned was rarely of good quality. The majority were impulse buys or from promotions. Clothes sales were my weakness. During the first cull of the wardrobe, numerous items that were donated still had tags on them. Many more had only been worn once or twice at most because I did not especially like them, the fit was a bit off, or the trend had come and gone. Sometimes, to be honest, the style looked downright ridiculous on me.

The stack of clothes removed so quickly from my wardrobe was embarrassing. In truth, most of these clothes should never have been bought in the first place. They served no purpose and had cost so much money, giving nothing in return. It was such a waste. I never wanted to find myself relapsing into this wasteful habit again. Bags and bags of clothes were folded and moved on to a better life. My wardrobe could breathe again.

It was during the second clear-out that I removed the last traditional suit that I owned. Placing it on the bed, I drank it in. It was a tailored one: jacket, skirt and pants, grey with delicate black piping at the edges. The coat had a peplum flick at the waist. The lining was a shimmering silver polka dot fabric. I had bought it years before because I thought I needed a suit. I didn't, but I felt like I should have one, just in case. Peplums had been popular at the time – almost everything had a flick at the waist in some shape or form. It was an elegant and well-made suit, but the truth was, I didn't like it, I had never liked it. I never felt comfortable in it.

When I bought it, I had just had my second child. I was tired, felt frumpy and had been at a low point emotionally. The suit felt uncomfortable because I had felt uncomfortable with myself. The result was that it had spent most of its life hidden in the wardrobe. I went out of my way not to wear it, but at the same time, I could not bring myself to part with it, it had cost so much. 'Surely someday it could come in useful,' I used to tell myself. That day was never going to come, not because peplum wasn't coming back but because I had attached so many negative thoughts to it. I was never going to relax in it. The dynamic this suit and I had was too ingrained to shake now, no matter how hard I tried. In its company, I felt tired, worn out and left behind. It was time to let it go.

I made a conscious effort to wear all the remaining clothes in my wardrobe after the second clear-out. Clothes that I had kept for good wear were worn on a routine basis. I felt better for this, as these tended to be more tailored, of a higher quality and better fit. I felt better while wearing them. Now I had fewer clothes to maintain and thus more time to give them the extra care required to keep them in good condition. As a result, almost everything that remained from that clear lasted nicely through the year and beyond.

THE UNAPPRECIATED WORLD OF THE COMFORTABLE SOCK

Of all the clothes that I learned to appreciate this year, one item stood out and that was the humble sock. I had never really rated socks up until then, they were just always in the press, with a fresh pair dragged out each morning. This formula had worked for years and would have continued to do so only for the issue that I began to run low on socks. They seemed to develop holes in their toes and heels at an alarming rate. I don't know if it was the additional walking, the outdoor lifestyle or unfortunate timing but they seemed to just all wear out in some sort of concerted team effort. Wearing odd socks became the norm and often I could be found sitting in the evening darning as best I could to make what I had last longer. The sight amused the kids, who cited various fairy tales where old women sat darning clothes by firelight; all I needed were glasses and an apron. Both of which I have, by the way, but I wasn't bringing that to their attention. They didn't need me to add fuel their fires.

I wasn't the only one to develop a new appreciation for socks this year. My son had outgrown his slippers, so off we went to procure new ones. Once out, we came across a cute packet of two pairs of green and blue fluffy slipper socks. They had a yeti design and silicone grippy bits on the soles. He was delighted, and couldn't wait to get home to try them on. As soon as we were in the door, he tore the remaining packaging away and donned the first pair, and for the rest of the evening he trotted around the house staring at his feet, pausing every now and again to wiggle his toes through the fluff. The action made the yeti's face come alive and this tickled him right to his core.

The joy that these simple socks brought surprised me – I hadn't realised that he had coveted socks like this for so long. He'd only ever seen his sister and me wear them and ours were sparkling pinks and creams and not something that he was willing to wear himself. Finding out that these socks were available in cool yeti form opened up a whole new world of experience for his feet. Many a Saturday evening, a row of fluffy winter slipper socks could be found dangling off our couch as we settled in for a family movie. So much comfort and enjoyment for such a small price.

KAREN MILLEN YOU'RE KILLING ME

Refraining from buying clothes and accessories wasn't the easiest and resulted in a few hairy moments. One in particular stands out. The coffee shop were my sister-in-law and I had arranged to meet was in a large shopping centre. One that I gave a wide berth to, to give my will power a fighting chance. Before the No-Spend Year, I happily spent hours browsing the shops and often used it to pass the time with the kids. The thought of spending time in one now was daunting.

Life could not be put on hold forever and I had to get used to living a normal life, doing normal things like normal people – and normal people go to shopping centres. After the coffee we were in good spirits and decided to browse. What harm could it do? There was nothing I needed urgently and it might be nice to indulge in a bit of window shopping.

All was going well until we entered a store where an exceptionally good sale was running. It was the handbag section that caught my eye, specifically one particular handbag. It was from a designer that I love and this particular bag was different and well-made, a beautiful dusky pink colour and 80 per cent off. I could feel my heart flutter when I saw the price, it was one of the few times in my life when I can say that it really was a steal. The leather was so soft and the finish exquisite. I held it and brushed my fingers over the soft straps. I put it on my shoulder and walked around the store. This was a timeless statement handbag that I could bring to any occasion for decades to come and would never feel out of place with. Oh Karen Millen, you genius, you!

Unable to take it off I kept it on as I looked at other items, trying to distract myself. I tried to rationalise that it was only a bag, but nothing could take my mind away from wanting it so badly. I found myself walking toward the till, but right at the last moment as the expectant cashier girl caught my eye, I pivoted away and continued wandering around the store. Eventually, my sister-in-law caught me by the shoulders, rolled her eyes and ordered me to either buy the thing or walk away. Besides, I was making the security guard nervous. I slumped as I took the bag off. My fingers trembled as I gave it one last hug goodbye and reluctantly placed it on the display counter. I still think about that bag to this day. I hope whoever bought it loves it as much as I still do.

By the end of the year I didn't have the range of clothes or accessories I had formerly had. However, I did have a new appreciation for good quality socks and well-made clothes, and my love for handbags remains. I don't need volumes of anything. A smaller number of well thought-out options will do just fine.

28

MINIMALISM GETS TESTED

I remember when we moved into our current home. It felt so big, relative to the super-small rented apartment we'd been in previously. The first time I walked the hallway I remember thinking, wow, this place is enormous. I imagined the acres of room and space, our space. I felt so free and easy, like I could breathe deeply and relax. The Japanese word 'ma' means 'the beauty of uncluttered space' and this was the first time I truly understood that word. And yes, uncluttered space is a beautiful thing, even if I only had it for a brief moment.

We'd hired a moving van to lug our possessions to our new home. As the boxes, bags and cartons were unloaded, I wondered if the delivery guys had arrived at the right address. It took two large vans to bring everything. Surely we did not own so many things. I thought there had to be some mistake. We had just come from the world's tiniest and coldest apartment. Where had this avalanche of stuff come from?

When I met my husband many years earlier, he had reduced his belongings to a single backpack, a passport and three pairs of black socks. He was also hours away from emigrating forever, but that is a story for another day. As for me, at that time, all my stuff could fit comfortably in my tiny Fiat Punto. What sort of explosion of material possessions had happened in the meantime?

Unfortunately, it wasn't a mistake: everything there belonged to us. After barely surviving the recession, heavily scarred, we had moved several times, chasing jobs and trying to find a home to call our own. A side effect of this was that my parents and some friends had kindly taken in several boxes of our possessions. It was only when everything was brought together that we realised just how much we had accumulated over time. When all our belongings were stacked together, it was an impressive sight indeed. Nothing had been missed since it had been packed, nor had I any recollection of the contents of all these boxes.

If you think this was enough to change me – it wasn't. I saw this as a challenge. I never step back from a good old-fashioned challenge; besides, I had a brand-new house just waiting to be filled. Over the next few days, I managed to load every press, wardrobe, and shelf. The plan was to come back at some stage and work through it all. This, of course, never happened.

It was when I began to question my life that I started to see all these objects for what they were: clutter. Most of the stuff that I squirrelled away when we moved in remained precisely where I had left it all those years before. Much of it was now buried deeper under new things that we had accumulated since the move.

My grand plans of sifting through everything and putting it all in order never came to anything. My home had turned from a haven into a storeroom where I was fast running out of space. A large proportion of its contents had no business being there and claimed no more significant reason for occupation other than that it had always been there. This was no longer a good enough excuse in my book. It was time to give this minimalism thing a real run for its money.

THE CLEAR-OUT BEGINS

I began to clear out each shelf press and cupboard with gusto. I donated old sofas, a steamer, speakers, pottery and cutlery sets. Why I ever thought that I needed three cutlery sets I will never know. Pots, pans, old toys, books and clothes were moved on to new homes. Many of these things came into my life without much thought and left in the same manner. They were purchased on sale, on impulse, or on a whim. None of it brought the value or life-changing results it promised. I packed it all up and sent it on its next adventure.

There were a few items that were hard to part with. The most notable was my beloved motorbike. I dearly loved that bike, it symbolised so much to me: putting on the leather gear, revving up the engine and rolling down the road on a summer's day. It's just the best feeling in the world for me. However, as much joy as the bike brought me, I had to compare it to my values and the reason why I was undertaking this No-Spend Year. It was expensive to insure and maintain, making it a costly line item in our budget. I knew that time with my kids was worth more than my bike, so away it had to go.

It took a couple of months to work through the house, to sort things and organise to pass things on in the most sustainable way possible. I didn't want to just throw everything into a skip, these things needed at least a second chance at life. So I developed a system of organising each item into a specific category. Anything that was staying required its own place in the house if it was not in use. Everything else was divided into sections for passing onto friends, donating, selling or repurposing. If an item didn't fit the criteria for the categories above, it was consigned to the bin, although this was kept as a last resort.

Many of my friends had young children and were happy to take the clothes, toys and other things that the kids had outgrown. Other items, many of which were either new or practically new, were easy to donate or sell. However, the final category before the landfill was a new one for me. It was the repurposing category. This category spawned several projects, including turning cool jars into retro drinking glasses. Pretty but old clothes were made into coasters, table mats or soft furnishings. Spray bottles got refilled with homemade lemon and vinegar cleaner.

One of the larger repurposing projects that we had was converting old clothes into T-shirt yarn. Clever YouTube videos showed us easy ways of using it for rug making and wall hangings, using simple knitting or crochet techniques. We created family projects and carefully designed personal pieces to decorate our home. Each item has particular memories attached to it, including, for example, a rug that was woven from our worn-out summer T-shirts. The colours remind us of trips and days out. These pieces are far from perfect, but that's what makes them special to us, and every time I walk our hallway, I catch a glimpse of them and smile.

Many things got repurposed. The majority were fun projects to do with the kids. They worked well to reduce the amount of waste we produced. The number of things bought was also reduced, giving us an extra boost in savings, alongside a slightly quirkier look for our home.

Our Home Became Ours

With all the extra items leaving, the house slowly but surely took shape. I began to relax and breathe deeply in my home, just like I had on the first day we arrived. Without realising it, I had become accustomed to the suffocating feeling of not being in control of our things. The contents of the house had been my master, demanding frequent cleaning and maintenance. I didn't realise how mentally suffocating it was to have unpacked boxes, trinkets and 'just in case' things on every shelf. By removing everything that didn't have a purpose, I was able to see and use the things that I did need. I learned to care for my things better and give what remained the respect it deserved. I wanted the things that were left in my home to work well and do the jobs that they were bought to do and not just be lost to the dark recesses of some cupboard.

29

MY DAUGHTER TAKES ON MINIMALISM AND WINS

As enamoured as I was with minimalism, not everyone in the household was on board with the changes. My daughter was particularly resistant. Minimalism was too abstract a concept for her to get her 8-year-old head around. I had spoken to her about minimalism and about how everything that we owned needed to bring value and have a function. In her room, everything did have value and purpose – for her – from the used bottle cap to a worn-out sock. So, when I approached her to help sort out her overflowing mess of a room, I was met with resistance. For a long time, I had left her bedroom alone. This suited me, as I had a whole house to work through. I hoped that by seeing minimalism in action in other places in the house, she would come to understand what I was trying to achieve.

She watched me as I worked my magic in the other rooms. Silently observing as I hauled out the contents of presses and cupboards, she saw me stack, sort and divide piles into categories. We would sometimes chat as I worked, with her lending a hand if the notion took her, or more likely when I directly asked for help. I hoped that, by involving her, I would help her get joy from this practice too. Ergo, when the time came to de-clutter her room, she would embrace the challenge and relish the satisfaction of clearing out most of its pointless contents.

One of the last places to get the minimalism treatment was the den. It was transformed from a small, cluttered storeroom to a useful space. I could work on my projects and the kids could make crafts, do jigsaws and play games with their friends. In the evenings, we'd turn on music and chat while we all worked on our individual projects. It was one of the best transformations in the whole house, and I figured that surely this would be enough to bring her over to the minimalist side.

When the time had come, I asked if we would sort out her room next. She responded with a simple brush-off: 'Maybe next time, Mom, it's fine for now.' This time I couldn't take no for an answer, there weren't any other rooms to work on; hers was the priority now. She dug her heels in, hard. I asked her why she was okay with every other part of the house being revamped and not her room. I thought that maybe it was because she was quite skilled at putting chores on the long finger or avoiding them entirely. She assured me that that was not it. I could see that she meant it. She said she liked the recent changes in the rest of the house but wanted her room to be left alone.

I needed to get to the bottom of this. We sat on my daughter's bed and had a long chat. It took her a while to articulate it, her big blue eyes brimming with tears. 'I don't know, Mom; I just don't want my stuff to be taken away.' She voice wavered as she struggled to put emotions she hadn't experienced before into words. She said she felt that anything outside her room was acceptable to change, move and apply minimalism to. However, when it came to her room, her personal space, having someone come in and change everything that she held dear didn't sit well. She felt that I didn't understand her, or the trinkets and keepsakes that were important to her.

The dilemma was clear. When we looked at my child's room, we saw it from two entirely different vantage points. I saw a jumbled-up mess. She saw her creative, safe place filled with projects and memories. I was her mother, and giving her a clean and tidy space to call her room was part of my job. However, how could it be her room if her personality wasn't allowed to be part of it? I could not expect her to grasp my life experiences and motivations for things when she has not lived my life. She has only lived her life, and if I wanted her to grow up strong-minded and independent, then I needed to listen to her point of view. This wasn't going to be easy, but there had to be a middle ground.

We sat in silence for a while, wondering how we were going to get through this impasse. Then a solution occurred to me. 'How about we give your room a makeover instead?' I suggested. 'We can create groups of things, one for keeping, one for giving away and one for the bin.'

'And what about the things that I am not sure about?' came the reply.

'Well, we'll just make a fourth pile for those things,' I replied. 'We'll store them in the top of your wardrobe. If you don't want anything in it for six months then we will donate it, what do you think?' There was a pause as she processed the proposition. She nodded in agreement, and we got to work. We gathered boxes to be filled, carefully labelling them, and put them in the hall outside her door. We worked diligently for the morning.

In the meantime, her brother, growing interested in the flurry of work, wanted in on the excitement too. Even though his room had been cleared up already, I gave his a cursory going over as well. He didn't own nearly as many things as his sister, but I did discover his fantastic ability to hide peanuts in the darkest recesses of his room. Even though his place had been totally revamped only a few weeks before, I found enough nuts to make a jar of peanut butter.

There's a striking difference between my two offspring with regard to their work ethic. My daughter was happy to do this job as a team, while her fair-weather brother only participated in a supervisory capacity. He sat perched on his locker, pointing out the various areas he wanted cleared up. If I suggested that he could be more productive by helping rather than pointing, he insisted that only I could do it properly. Rather than waste energy negotiating, I just kept going, and soon his room was as good as it was going to get. So with a strict warning that no food was allowed, especially not behind skirting boards or in sock drawers, I headed over to spend the rest of my time helping my daughter.

It took us most of that day to negotiate the final version of her room. Seeing my daughter's new surroundings, with the cute seating area and her desk adorned with a hoard of fluffy pens and coloured stationery, I could see her personality coming through. She was growing into herself, and it was clear that her character was going to be a strong one. I was proud of her and the number of toys she'd let go of. I kept my word and stored the 'maybe' box high up in her wardrobe, and we stacked the donate box by the door for the next time we were in town. I told her if she was happy to keep her room like this, then come next summer she could pick out new curtains and paint to really put her own stamp on it. 'Really? How about black and red?' she beamed as she whizzed around with craft paper, scissors and pencils to create a mood board for her room's new look. 'We'll see,' I replied, secretly hoping that she would change her mind by then. From then until now, the room has been kept tidy; a low level of tidiness, but a level, nonetheless. She is happier in her personal space, and so am I. If it is red she chooses then so be it, she's earned it. Although I draw the line at black.

THE GIRL'S ETHOS RUBS OFF

I love the aspirational images of huge windows with voile curtains, everything pristine white and bright. A single lush green potted plant adorns a sleek steel corner table and there is very little else in the room. I've been known to covet magazine photographs like this and have dreamed of similar spaces being mine. However, gazing at my girl bent over her desk, designing her new room scheme, made me think more about our own home and what our home's personality was. Just then something dawned on me. I didn't covet the magazine rooms anymore. I can't, a place like that would be entirely incongruent with our lives.

This gave me an idea. I made my way down the hall and opened the storage box that contained some crystal glasses we had received as a wedding gift. The box sat alongside a beautiful cutlery set that I kept for Christmas and dinner parties. Of the three spare sets that I had accumulated, I had held this one back during the January clean-out, as I hadn't been ready to part with it just yet. I thought about how beautiful they were and what a shame it was that they were so rarely used. The craftsmanship that had gone into them was apparent. Here they were, hidden away, never to be admired. They might as well not exist, and that was a shame.

Taking a leaf from my girl's book, I picked up both boxes and marched to the kitchen with them. I took out and polished each glass, then sat them in the glass-door cupboard, ready for use. I was going to enjoy drinking out of these, and each time I would remember my wedding day and remind myself of how lucky I was to have the family I do.

I repeated the polishing process on the cutlery. We were forever running low on spoons and forks. Often I would hand one of the kids a tea towel before dinner asking them to dry the cutlery that I had retrieved from the dishwasher and washed so that we had enough for the meal. Extra cutlery had been on my list of things to get. It now seemed like an absurd purchase in light of having such a good quality set sitting there gathering dust.

That evening we ate dinner using the new cutlery and drank from the crystal glasses. It made dinner feel extra special, even though it was a simple mid-week family meal. The knives cut easily, and the glasses clinked. It was a simple pleasure but an important reminder to me to use what I have and not save things up for that special occasion. Today was special enough.

30

COFFEE AND COOKBOOKS

One day I took a mid-afternoon break and sat for a few minutes to gather my thoughts over a cup of coffee with two spoons of coffee and a good splash of milk. We have two swivel chairs in the kitchen with a small wooden coffee table in between. I remember the day we bought those chairs. I thought that they looked like something out of the 1960s. My husband fell in love with them straight away.

The thing is, I don't ever think that he saw how ugly they were. I believe he saw that they would fit in our kitchen and give him somewhere to sit that was not the kitchen table chairs. My dear husband cuts a very slim figure and as a result finds sitting on hard surfaces for any time to be quite uncomfortable. I have to say there is a certain charm about having things that are ugly and ill-fitting in a room. To be fair, they are quite comfortable to sit in – pretty much perfect for a coffee break.

WHO AM I?

While sipping the coffee, my eyes fell on my bulging cookbook shelf. I smiled. They gave me a sense of achievement and spoke of the type of person I felt that I should be. These books said that I was interesting, well-travelled, enjoyed learning new things and experimenting with new tastes. These books told any visitor that I was a good mother, that I cooked exotic foods for my children, developing their budding palates and opening their eyes to a world of tastes and aromas. This shelf also spoke to the type of partner I was, it indicated that I had a growth mindset and that I cared. They also said that I was exciting and worth being friends with. If I got rid of them because of some dalliance with being a minimalist, how could anyone possibly know what type of person I was?

Furthermore, these books implied that they were in use and played an essential part in my everyday life, if they held such pride of place in my kitchen and were so high in number. What sort of creature would give over such valuable real-estate on a kitchen shelf if not for something of significance in the daily running of this critical part of the home? It would be folly for it to be any other way.

I had given my cookbooks a wide berth when it came to the minimalist side of things. My reasoning was that I do genuinely love cooking and staring at these books – imagining the dishes hidden inside makes me smile. I never thought at the start of this year that these beauties would come close to the firing line. Yet here I was, sipping my coffee and staring at their bright spines and wondering ... what if they succumbed to minimalism? These books that I held dear to my heart now seemed different. Now the sheer volume of books seemed excessive and almost gluttonous. Yet at the same moment, they were part of my identity.

I stood up and padded over to the shelf, running my fingers along the spines, carefully reading each title as a fingertip pressed against it. I could feel the conflict rising inside of me as it dawned on me that I did not buy many of these books myself. Worse still, I had not used most of these books in a very long time. Maybe never. I kept them as a symbol of my love of food and cooking. I kept them for my vanity and ego. They represented part of who I was to the world.

This reputation was so strong that I received many books as presents from well-meaning friends. Titles were chosen for me and not by me. Each of these books fed my arrogance. The arrogant part of me that shouted what a great mother and wife I was. I am educated in world cuisines, and I have travelled and have great skill in understanding this intricate world of taste.

DECISION TIME

The truth is I do love food, and I love to cook, but I'm no chef. Most of the books before me had not contributed to that love. They played little part in the depth of knowledge that I had and did not display any substantial part of my deep love of food and eating. They were window dressing, 'for display purposes only' so to speak, a sign of my errant affluence.

There and then I made a decision. These squatters had to go. I worked my way through the shelf, and one by one picked out every book that I had not used in the last three months. I stacked them on the kitchen table. What an impressive stack it was.

Before I lost my resolve, I quickly put them up for sale. Once I pressed the sell button, a little voice in my head screamed at me, asking what I thought I was up to. Caring people in my life had given me some of these books, and I had spent my hard-earned money on many others. Had I lost my marbles altogether? Cooking was pretty much my favourite pastime. Had I pushed the minimalism thing just a bit too far? Would I find myself scouring the internet to repurchase these books in just a few short days? The answer was simple. I didn't know.

Cookbooks are funny things. They hold a lot of emotion for people, myself included. Of all the things that I have given away this year, these books were among the hardest. Thankfully, the buyers of these books have shown gratitude in receiving them. One woman even hugged me as she had looked for a particular one for ages. That did feel good and took the sting out of my loss. Now that the books have moved onto their next life, the emotional bond between the materialistic world and me has weakened a little further. I feel lighter as a result. I look at the unburdened shelf now and still get the same sense of satisfaction from the small select stack as I did from the armada that existed before.

Each one of the remaining books has taught me something. Each of the remaining books is regularly consulted. It's obvious from the worn covers, looser spines and smudged pages. These are the books that I'll use to teach my children. They make me smile and bring value to my life. However, the one that holds pride of place is my grandmother's 1954 cookbook. It is held together with tape and string, there are few pictures, but there is more cooking history hidden in those pages than all my other books combined.

More books or fewer books, I am a person who loves to cook. I will always be a person who loves to cook and experiment with food. Whether I own zero cookbooks or a thousand cookbooks, I will still feel the same about the subject. I will always love the scent of freshly baked bread, the aroma of crushed spices. The power of these smells is unrelated to the number of books I own. They do not care if I am a minimalist or a hoarder. My ability to cook is not impaired by the removal of several under-utilised hardbacks from my kitchen, but focusing on the remaining books that I do love to cook from will make me better over time.

I have not ruled out future purchasing of cookbooks, but what I will do from now on is to use my local library as a test to see if a new book deserves a place in my kitchen. I will check it out to see if I warm to the recipes. Then, and only then, will it have a chance to be bought and gain a precious spot on my lovely kitchen cookbook shelf.

My need to pretend to be someone I'm not has been taken down a notch, yet I am still me. Dare I say that becoming a minimalist is moulding me into a better version of myself? I do not feel the need to make my kitchen or associated books remarkable. I do not have to prove anything to anyone but myself. It is the food that will come from my kitchen, and the coffee I make for friends and family, that will make it remarkable. Nothing more and nothing less. That is fine by me.

31

THE STAYCATION

For many years, we took our holidays with friends. It was a tradition that began before the kids were born. We would travel around Europe and sometimes further afield, often roughing it in the way only youth and naivete can allow. As time passed, we grew from couples into families, and annual vacations continued, although there was one notable change in our trips away. When kids came along, the yearly foreign holiday morphed into an Irish staycation.

Between us, we have five kids, four boys and one girl, all under ten years of age. Taking vacations with a group of nine was a project in itself. However, the No-Spend Year added an extra layer of complexity, to put it mildly. I briefly considered not going on holiday at all. Although that was quickly scrapped, this was a mindful spending year, not a cut-out-all-the-fun year. For the numbers to be realistic and sustainable, the year had to be comparable in as many ways as possible to every other year. Part of that was to ensure that we had a great family holiday. After some research and conversation, we decided to repeat the holiday we had had in 2018, as it would help to keep the number accurate. Additionally, the previous year's holiday had been so much fun that we were all happy to do it again.

Nevertheless, there were some significant considerations that I had to consider. I had no idea how this trip was going to work out with the new rules in place. How was I going to be able to keep up with a week of family entertainment on a minimal budget, without ruining another family's holiday? It was all well and good me taking part in this challenge, it was my choice after all. However, when it impacted our best friends, well, that was a different story. I was still finding my groove with the children and No-Spend Days; how could I incorporate a whole other family?

Moreover, would they want to be part of this crazy scheme? How was I going to stick to the €100 per week food budget and keep it fair? Finally, I had never been on a holiday where I didn't have a glass of wine at some stage, this would be a first. These thoughts stressed me out quite a bit, to say the least.

In the run-up to the holiday, the kids saved up their pocket money and did extra chores around the house to earn a little bit more. We also added a little extra for good behaviour. The holiday pocket money rule was that I couldn't interfere with how the money was spent. If they wanted ice-cream at 8 a.m. then they could get it. The only limitation was that the money they spent on the first day was the maximum they could spend for the whole week. They were delighted and spent hours planning which comics, toys and sweets they would buy. The anticipation in the house was palpable. Both delighted in the idea that they might annoy their mom with choco-late-covered faces first thing in the morning. To them this was utopian, and any financial limitation was worth it to see my disapproving eyerolls. The only big item bought in the run-up to the holiday was a new wet suit for my daughter, as she had outgrown her old one. Having a dependable wetsuit is a big priority for us. A quality wetsuit allows the kids to spend all day on an Irish beach in comfort. My son fitted nicely into his sister's old one and was delighted with the bright stripes on it.

Typically, I visited the hair and nail salon before any trip away. I would invest in a new holiday wardrobe and all the associated accessories. Not this year. This year, I rummaged through my closet and worked with what I had. In the end, it wasn't too bad. I did have some cute summer clothes, most of which hadn't seen the light of day since last summer. These would get me respectably through the holiday, I thought to myself. I did toy with the idea of wearing makeup on the beach but knowing that I would be in a wet suit for most of it, I had to concede that a full face of makeup would be a step too far (wouldn't it?). I decided to pare back my makeup complement to the bare minimum of mascara and tinted moisturiser.

The accommodation was a five-bedroomed self-catering house, which we booked for the last week in June before the prices went up for the high season in July and August. The year before we had booked the first week in July, just as the rate went up. Booking the house only one week earlier allowed us to take advantage of the off-peak price. That was one significant saving, the two other big outgoings were food and entertainment. These would need planning. It was time to see what I could do to find that balance of having fun and eating well without it costing a fortune.

LET THE FUN BEGIN

As we pulled up to the house, I was still a bit apprehensive about the week ahead. We quickly unpacked our things. It had been a long journey, and we needed to let off some steam. The kids flung on their wet suits and swimwear, and we all raced to the beach.

Their excitement was tangible. I, however, was still mentally holding back, worrying about maintaining the integrity of my experiment while making sure that everyone had a great holiday. On the beach, I took my friend aside and explained my concerns about the restrictions on spending. She had been well aware of what I was doing but this was the first time that she had had to deal with it directly.

As with so many other times in my life, my concerns were unfounded. It turned out that she was delighted with my idea of combining money into a kitty for food for the families. Thankfully, my friend was a fantastic cook, and with her three growing boys, eating out all the time was just not a possibility anyway, so my idea of combining €100 per family into a kitty for food for the week was happily embraced. There were several supermarkets and local shops close by, so with a bit of planning food-wise we were looking good. I was feeling optimistic. €200 for the week should comfortably get us by. Eating at home and having picnics was a more relaxed and fun way to feed our little army.

For the whole seven days, we had a ball. In the mornings we had cereal, toast, juice, fruit, bagels and coffee. Lunches became the high point. We would pack a picnic and head off to the beach, mountains, trail, play-park or wherever took our fancy. When it was lunchtime or 'egg sandwich time' as it quickly became known, I would whip out the trusty camp stove and frying pan. The kids would cut shapes with cookie cutters in the middle of a slice of bread. The bread was then placed in the pan, and an egg cracked into the centre. It is the perfect afternoon treat, and the kids lined up for them. Afterwards, we would break open the nuts, seeds, fruit, popcorn or sweeter snacks for them to round out the lunch before running off for another session on the swings.

The week was full of noise and laughter, there was always something going on. At times we would break into smaller groups to go cycling, while others would check out a new beach, go for cliff walks, hunt for sea glass or follow a fairy maze. We had a boule set, which made for hours of entertainment wherever we went. There was always a cooler bag full of snacks and treats to be enjoyed.

In the evenings, we took turns cooking while the kids played cards, board games or more often we all headed down to the beach again for another swim or sandcastle-making session. Once the kids were in bed, and there was still plenty of light in the evening, a couple of us would don our wet suits again and head down to dive off the higher rocks. After that, we'd swim around the head, by inlets and small bays and back to shore. Those evening swims were one of the high points of the trip, especially when it was just my husband and me. It was our time – we chatted and caught up with each other after the day's events, as kayaks and surfers glided by. In the distance, we could see figures picking shells and stones in the coves. It was our little world, just us, surrounded by the beautiful coast and open sea. Once back we would put on some music and play poker as a group until the early hours.

The kids didn't notice any difference in that year's holiday, as there were plenty of treats and tasty things to eat all the time, between what we bought from the food budget and their own allowance. It was agreed that having autonomy over their own money made every ice-cream buying moment an event in itself. The freedom and trust meant more to them than me buying treats and doling them out at my discretion. They felt so grown up, and in reality, they actually ate fewer sweets during that holiday than on any other holiday. They still talk about the time they bought the raspberry sorbet with the tutti-frutti ice-cream topped with sprinkles and everything else the poor store owner could pile on top of the cone. My daughter now makes eggy bread for both her and her brother on Saturday mornings, delighted with her newfound culinary skills.

THE SAME BUT DIFFERENT

We took other trips during the year; however, they were mainly day trips to historical monuments, local parks and other such fun places. That camping stove came with us on every single one of them. I almost felt like getting it a booster seat to take pride of place in the back with the kids. That stove had started out the year like so many other things I'd bought on a whim years before. It gathered dust in our garage for so long and it was only now that I see the great value that it brings to us. The kids never seem to tire of it, and warm food mixed with fresh air is such a refreshing combination.

That holiday ended up costing a full total of €602 per family for the week. This included accommodation, food, entertainment, a new wet suit for my girl and one lunch out on the last day. The meal out felt like a special treat to round off a lovely trip. We all enjoyed it. In 2018, the same stay had totalled €1,257. This was over double the cost for the same holiday. The additional expenses were mainly eating out, take-away food, coffees, entrance into activities and holiday clothes. Lovely as these things were, cutting back on them made absolutely no difference to our enjoyment of the trip. I didn't miss my makeup or new clothes at all. I am glad to say that my worries about the trip were unfounded.

However, the financial difference was significant. I don't remember having a better time the year before – in fact, I do remember worrying about paying off the credit card the following month. The 2018 holiday ate our savings, with nothing noteworthy about it to justify almost double in the cost. This time, none of us had to worry about the upcoming credit card bills, and the total amount was quite manageable for a week-long fun-packed family holiday.

32

POCKET MONEY

I decided to give the kids autonomy over their pocket money. Now was as good a time as any to get them used to handling their own money. This meant that they would both receive the equivalent of their age in pocket money each week, provided they completed their chores adequately. Every Saturday morning, my daughter received €8, and my son €5. As their birthdays came around, the amount went up by €1. Also, any money from birthdays or other special occasions would be kept by them as theirs.

From my perspective, this was a lot of money to put in a young child's hand each week, and it was unfair to give them that responsibility without some guidance attached. Let's face it, if I had been handed that sort of money as a kid, I would have dropped it all immediately at the local sweet shop. I would have gobbled the whole lot down before I even reached home, making myself ill in the process, inevitably leaving me with nothing to my name until the following pocket money day, where I would repeat the cycle all over again. I know my kids, and that apple did not fall far from the tree when it came to money and treats. That was not how I wanted to introduce them to cash, nor was it how I wanted to spend my Saturdays. I wanted to give them freedom with their money, but that freedom came with guidelines. Those guidelines came in the form of the Three Jar Money System.

We started one afternoon in early January, when I called both cherubs into the kitchen and sat them at the table. After placing three washed, clean jars in front of each of them, I asked them to decorate and customise the jars using their favourite markers. The labels were: Spending, Saving and Charity.

Squeals of delight rose from the dining table. They didn't know yet what I was up to, but, they had cottoned on to the fact that it involved receiving money. Money was a massive bonus in their book, so they decorated with enthusiasm. Interestingly, the Spending jar seemed to get the lion's share of the decoration.

Once the jars were finished and lined up with pride, I explained that I would not be buying sweets or toys for them – this year they were going to be in control of that themselves. They would receive pocket money each week and any money that they received for birthdays or other events would be divided out between the jars. I could not play any part in how the money was spent; however, they were limited to what was in their jar and their jar alone. This brought on further yelps of excitement. I could almost see the sugar bubbles rising from their heads. It sounded like bliss to them. That was until I explained what each jar was for and how the money was to be divided out.

THE SPENDING JAR

The Spending jar is for living in the now. With this money they could buy whatever they liked and spend it however they wanted to. From experience I knew that this money would be quickly exchanged for sugared confectionery. As much as I didn't want them having too much junk food, I preferred for them to be able to buy sweets themselves, so I would not be giving in and randomly purchasing them for them when we were out. It was up to them to treat themselves as they saw fit. It also allowed them to feel like they were getting something for doing their chores during the week. Saving money at their age with no immediate reward was too big an ask. So it was with the greatest of delight that my children committed to spending that money every week. It was in the rules, after all. This jar took 20 per cent of the money.

THE SAVING JAR

The Saving jar was going to be a significant one for all of us this year. Since I was having a No-Spend Year, I had to keep tight control of our discretionary spending. This meant that unless it was an item that we needed, I had to refrain from spending money. Buying toys and treats at random was out of the question. Even though my kids did not know it at the time, this jar would be a game-changer for them. The money that was to go into this jar was not to save up for college or long-term things that I would teach them about later. For now, all I needed was for them to grasp the concept of delayed gratification and the satisfaction of saving up for something they wanted. This jar was for any toys, games or experiences that they wanted. It took 70 per cent of the pocket money.

THE CHARITY JAR

The Charity jar is my personal favourite, although it took a bit of explaining before the kids got their heads around it. The money that was put in there goes to a charity of the child's choice. For me, it is vital to nurture generosity in my children and help them to understand that there is a lot of good to be done in this world, no matter what your means. It was also a roundabout way of introducing the tax system to them. Even though they were receiving a set amount per week, a certain amount had to be given away and was not for them to keep. This jar commanded 10 per cent of their money.

The first time they donated to charity, it was to a local animal shelter. They picked the shelter themselves, and we rang ahead to make sure that they were open. The owners of the sanctuary were lovely, and they kindly showed the kids around so that they could meet all the animals and learn about how the poor things ended up there in the first place. Both were enthralled and left the shelter chattering about how they were going to save up more money to donate again. After that, they were hooked.

As I couldn't entirely abdicate my fiscal responsibilities as a parent, I did list out the things that I would be paying for throughout the year. Anything school-related, clothes, sports etc. would be my responsibility. These were all important things that the kids loved being involved in, and I felt they were too important to give up for a whole year.

33

HOW THE KIDS GOT THE BETTER OF THE
NO-SPEND YEAR

About halfway through the year, my daughter got it into her head that she wanted a tablet to play games on. I had absolutely no intention of introducing such a device to my children, mainly since my daughter was only eight. She felt hard done by because the previous Christmas Santa had presented several kids in her class with iPads and other tablet devices. I had explicitly vetoed electronics from Santa's wish list, explaining that Santa hadn't a hope of building such sophisticated electronics up at the North Pole. Having lost that battle and had Santa make a complete liar out of me, I had to think of something else.

I came up with what I thought was the most cunning of plans. I told my girl that I couldn't possibly justify buying such items this year because of the No-Spend Year. If she really wanted one, then she had to save up for it entirely herself. I was delighted at having bought myself another year, not thinking for a moment that she would ever get the funds needed to pay for one. As far as I was concerned, the whole idea was put to bed. More fool me. Little did I know that my darling daughter saw this as a green light.

Over the next few months, she squirrelled away and saved as much as she could, often forgoing her spending money without so much as a grumble. She knew that if she complained, I would try to put a stop to her plan and dissuade her. My daughter beavered away, funnelling everything she possibly could into her kitty. In the run-up to her birthday, she pre-empted most people by asking for money instead of gifts. My parents and other good-natured relatives agreed and promptly paid up in cash, which she carefully stashed away.

After exhausting all her financial avenues, including requesting extra chores that she felt sorely underpaid for, she was still short some of the money she needed. This left her stumped for a while and a little disheartened. Watching her, I was conflicted. I'd never seen this side of her before. I wanted so badly for her to succeed, considering the effort she was putting in. However, I didn't want her to reach her goal as that would mean I couldn't stop her getting that tablet. So far, the dream of the tablet was just far enough out of reach that I could sleep easy.

That was until she struck upon a plan that surprised even me. She decided to run a raffle in our local area, with a prize of a voucher for Kildare Village Shopping outlet. She put together flyers and printed them out, detailing everything about the raffle, why she was doing it, what the prize was and when the draw would happen. She bought a small ticket book and made me drive her to the shopping village to get the voucher. She did all of this herself, teaching herself the rudiments of Microsoft Office in the process. Once everything was arranged, she spent every afternoon for the next week cycling around our neighbourhood selling her raffle tickets. Her enthusiasm was infectious and soon she had her younger brother out knocking on doors with her.

She did well, and I have to hand it to our lovely neighbours, who got into the spirit of what my child was up to. One particular evening she came home asking me, 'What is an entrepreneur, Mom? I keep being called an entrepreneur, is that a bad thing? And why do they keep saying it?' I explained to her that an entrepreneur was a person who started and ran their own business. After considering this, she responded, 'That's nice, maybe when I'm older, and I want more tablets to play on'. Off she skipped to figure out her running total.

On the day of the raffle, we stood outside our gate with cordial, cookies and a big bucket full of tickets sitting on a small picnic table beside us. When the time came to draw the winner, the crowd did a big drum roll, and one other neighbour pulled out the winning ticket with a flourish. There was clapping and excitement all around.

That evening a wad of money was put on the table in front of me. 'I know which one I want to get, Mom, can we get it now?' she was beaming with pride. She had the right amount of money down to the cent. I was caught – how could I refuse after she had put in so much effort? The following morning we climbed into the car and headed to the computer store. She walked straight up to the store clerk and listed off the exact specifications for the tablet that she wanted, 'Ideally in a rose gold finish if possible, please,' she finished. The clerk looked at me with humour and surprise and I shrugged my approval, something that I find myself doing a lot when it comes to that girl. The clerk returned a few moments later with the requested tablet and talked her through everything thoroughly, throwing some hints and tips into the mix. The two them got deep into conversation about gigabytes and screen quality. In the car on the way home, between squeals of delight and excitement, she reassured me that she would stick strictly to the rules of use and to be fair to her she has been commendable in that department.

FAST LEARNING CONTINUES

As the year wore on, we fell into a routine. The kids adjusted to the new way of being. I tried hard to swap out spendy habits for less spendy habits. However, scenarios did come up where I felt that spending money was indeed a good idea. One of these was the annual book fair, held in our local school.

I firmly believe in supporting our local school. It is especially useful when these things have a win-win result, and the school book fair is the perfect sweet spot for that. The kids get to choose from a great selection of books, and the proceeds go to the school. In the days coming up to the book fair each year, the excitement in our house is palpable. The kids pore over the book fair leaflet, highlighting some of their choices, and debates about who was going to get what could be heard bouncing off the walls. I usually allow them to pick out several books and just hand over the amount required. However, this year I had to slow down and think about how I was going to do this.

We were already so lucky with the local public library, school library and an ample number of books at home. There was little need for brand-new books. As avid a reader as I was, the No-Spend Year rules, along with minimalism, dictated that purchases like this had to be thought through.

To find a balance, I decided that I would allow them to buy one book, with two caveats attached. The first was that it had to be a reading book that was just above their current reading level. The second was that the maximum amount the book should cost was €10. They had to come to me with their thought-out choices and only then would I give them the money. Finally, they had to buy the book themselves and figure out the change, if any.

They ran with this challenge. My daughter knows me like the back of her hand and understood straight away how to work the system. She returned to me two days later with a handwritten letter explaining the reasons as to why she wanted her particular book, which was €11.20. I've seen business plans with less effort put into them than this submission. She went to great lengths to tell me why – even though the book was over the maximum allowance – the benefits that she would receive from it far exceeded any additional costs.

My son, being six, got somewhat bogged down by the challenge – he was easily distracted by the pencils and sticker books on offer. Eventually he settled on one book for €3.70. I asked him if he was sure and to work out the change from €10 before I handed over the money. He came back about ten minutes later requesting a set of four books featuring the same characters, for €9.90. I believe he had sought his older sister's help on that one.

The boy stretched the rule of only one book but stayed under the limit, and the girl extended her financial budget but stayed within the number limit. For the effort that they both put in to get what they wanted, I couldn't but concede to them. I was really starting to enjoy how they were thinking laterally and figuring out how to get what they wanted. This was a far cry from the spendy babies I had created before this year.

The excitement that was in the house when they found out that I was going to let them have their choices was palpable. I have never seen them enjoy a set of books more than they did those. They have always enjoyed reading, but this was on a whole new level. I had to restrain myself from telling them to buy what they wanted; I had to let them enjoy the fruits of their labour. I knew that if I did give them free rein after all their efforts, it would take away from their success. These books were hard-won and well earned. More enjoyment was gleaned from the challenge than in all the previous hundred books that went through our home.

IN THEIR STRIDE

There were several other things that the kids really took in their stride during the year, particularly during the summer. With all the extra time outside, we took it upon ourselves to really get competent with cycling on the road. We learned the rules of the road, and over time we've been able to take further and further trips away from home. The kids embraced this new hobby with enthusiasm. I, on the other hand, am far from a natural when it comes to these things. It took several trips and much coaxing from the group to get me to take on the more daring parts of the adventures, like crossing roads and navigating potholes. This naturally left me on the receiving end of many jokes.

Often after a long day out in the fresh air, a cinema evening would be called for. We would close the curtains, make some popcorn, debate energetically who got to pick the movie and then would settle in a heap together for an evening's viewing. This was one of my favourite ways to spend a day, fluffy socks and all.

The other projects that we took on included dusting down the keyboard in our garage. I had inherited it from my sister-in-law and the back was bashed to bits, and it's a bit rusty on the speakers, but once it was cleaned down my son was delighted to spend time learning the basics. I did make a mental note to maybe invest in some headphones for him for Christmas, though. I also offered up my sewing machine, as the older one had been showing an interest, so I taught her how to thread it up and gave her some old clothes to cut up and play around with. After some rocky starts, she's starting to get the hang of it, and if my boy shows an interest too, I'll teach him, too.

BACK TO SCHOOL

The kids going back to school as a whole exercise in itself. I am fortunate with my school because there is an excellent book rental scheme in place. We just pay a certain fee per child and all their books, copies and supplies are covered. However, there was also the stationery and school bag situation to deal with. A stationary list came in from the school and I could feel another spending spree coming on. The kids insisted that they had to have everything on the list, but I wasn't going to the shops without a clear list of what we really needed. One of the most useful skills I learned this year was the power of making a list and sticking to it. So one August Thursday morning I called the kids to the kitchen table, placed snacks on it, and with pen and paper in hand, we got to work.

We gathered all their lunch boxes, crayons, pencils and bags. My son's school bag was torn through. My daughter had been given a new school bag from her uncle for her birthday. Her old one was in excellent condition and had the added benefit of being a Pokémon one, so her brother was more than happy to inherit it from her. We topped and sorted all kinds of pencils and markers until they were pleased with what they had. There was some trading back and forth of specific colours and styles, and lunch boxes were agreed upon. It took the entire morning, but by lunchtime we had most everything sorted. In the end, the only things that we needed were a pencil case for the girl and whiteboard markers for both.

As it turned out, the pencil case sorted itself out – a neighbour who had older daughters and several pencils that were no longer in use was happy to allow her to pick one. She was delighted – the one she got was an eye-watering pink and scented, a dream come true for a little girl. Not only did we get organised for school that morning, but we got to finally put some manners on that colouring box of theirs.

34

NO ALCOHOL FOR AN ENTIRE YEAR

Probably the hardest thing to put on the manifesto was abstaining from alcohol. It nearly didn't make it on at all – not because I didn't think that it would have an impact but because I knew that it would really test me. I was the typical New Year's resolution: best intentions followed by swift and epic failure. I was the one who would resolve to change her life every January: I would bin junk food and make my credit card cry with new work-out gear and supplements, only to fall flat on my face and give up a week in, bitter at my own failure and feeling more defeated than ever.

I was reluctant to embrace sobriety for an entire year. A little voice in my head sniped how unnecessary it was to take such drastic action. Then again, was not dyeing my hair or buying clothes not also in that same radical category? I knew that it might be the right thing to do, but I am selfish and am liable to do selfish things. I can also be a chicken and guilty of cowardice from time to time. This was one of those times. I just didn't know if I was strong enough to buck the habit of a lifetime or turn my back on our drinking culture. For a long time it was not on the manifesto and I negotiated internally to maybe only drink once a month or adopt some other more lenient version. I was looking for any excuse or exemption just to avoid a flat-out drinking ban. Despite my internal rationalisations, three things combined to push me to commit.

THE PUSH

Firstly, one evening while watching a *Simpsons* episode with the kids, Bart spiked his teacher's drink. She got drunk in school and was subsequently fired. My daughter, puzzled, asked, 'Mom, why did he do that? Now she's lost her job.' I replied that Bart had done this as a trick because he thought it was funny, but had meant no harm by it. She was dismayed – not only that someone could get another person drunk, but that a person might willingly do it to themselves. I, at the time, happened to have a glass of wine beside me. On hearing his sister, my son turned to me, pointed to the glass and said, 'That will "drunk" you, Mom, it's bad.' Two big sets of eyes stared at me, bringing a wave of shame with them. What message was I sending my children? I focus so much on their health, helping them to build active bodies and minds, yet they see me wantonly damaging mine.

The second thing was that when out, my well-meaning friends would insist on buying me a drink, just as I would for them. This year I would not be able to buy one back. This would change the balance of my friendships, which was something I definitely did not want. Neither would it be in the spirit of the year. This year was about living better and saving money, not mooching off others and spreading my costs around to everyone else.

Finally, giving up alcohol would have a direct impact on the numbers. A simple bottle or two of wine between us per week is about €20. Over a year, this amounts to €1,040 of post-tax money. Add in Christmas, birthdays, nights out and gifts and I feel that I can modestly double that number. This would hit the bottom line by over €2,080 per year. That would be before the spin-off costs – the mixers, glasses, taxis, hotel stays, late-night takeaways, meals, and goodness knows what else. This amount alone would cover a large proportion of the household running costs for a year. It was too big a line item not to be addressed. This was going to be the longest stretch that I had ever had without alcohol since I was about fourteen years old. In fact, I guessed that, pregnancies aside, even a month without having a drink might have won that title up until now.

Four short days into the No-Spend Year I met some friends for a night out. I was nervous as heck about my ability to get past the first month, let alone an entire year. Most reasonable people would have given the social scene a wide berth for the first few weeks at least, yet here I was, in a bar, surrounded by pints, food and loud music. I had to keep reminding myself that I was there to enjoy my friends' company but, I wasn't doing that. I was busy battling my old habits, wanting to be part of the merriment. I wanted to join in with a drink in my hand like everyone else. That was the night that I realised that FOMO was real. Maybe I could call a halt to this now, I thought, before this bid for sobriety was common knowledge. If nobody knew that I failed then nobody could judge me. Anyway, doesn't everyone fail in their New Year's resolutions? Why should this be any different?

It was just when I was about to concede defeat that a friend leaned in and said something that I'll never forget. 'Well done, you, this will change your entire relationship with alcohol, we could all do with a bit of that.' She squeezed my hand and gave me one of her fantastic warm smiles.

I never really thought about alcohol in any specific terms, especially not in terms of a relationship. I just drank sometimes, it's a thing that most people do, like breathing or making your bed. It was not a great achievement, nor was it a burden. It just was. When she said it, something stirred and I knew she was right. I didn't realise just how right she was at the time. Her words at that moment are something that I am still grateful for, which made all the other comments of, 'I couldn't do that,' and 'A whole year, are you mad?!' fade into the background. It was in that moment, feeling the squeezing of my hand combined with that genuine and supportive smile, that I knew I wasn't going to give up. I was going to give this my best shot.

With the whirlwind of minimalism, budgets and No-Spend Days of January, I made it through my first month without drinking. It went by so much faster than I had anticipated, lulling me into a false sense of security and making me think I had this not-drinking thing well in hand. This year would be a dawdle.

That was until I met February. I make no bones about my dislike of February – it is a dark, cold and wet month at the best of times. A month tagged on to the end of an already long winter. This was when I found giving up alcohol the hardest, for more reasons than I had anticipated. February was when my husband was admitted to the hospital. It was also when my resolve was tested to the absolute limit.

UNEXPECTED CRISIS

After seventeen hours in A&E crippled with pain, he was diagnosed with atypical appendicitis. You would think that after 42 years his appendix would have made a home for itself and not be looking for an eviction, but no, that appendix had ideas of its own. Surgery was scheduled for first thing in the morning.

It was almost midnight when I turned the key in the door. I shivered as I turned the heating on and my footsteps echoed as I went to hang up my jacket. My limbs were heavy, my brain was muddled, but I couldn't sleep just yet. The antiseptic scent of the hospital lingered on my clothes. A grim reminder that my husband was lying there in pain and all on his own. I showered and settled myself into his chair, nursing a cup of tea. As I watched the steam rising, everything around me felt so different, so empty. I had never spent an evening on my own in our house before. I was always with him or the kids, usually both. A wave of loneliness washed over me, all at once, and I was overcome. The tension of the longest day descended hard. What would I do if anything happened to him tonight or on the operating table tomorrow? I would be lost without him.

The steaming tea did not bring the comfort that I was looking for. I pulled down a bottle of wine and lifted a crystal glass from the shelf. I padded back to the sitting room, uncorked the thing and poured myself a glass. I stared at that burgundy liquid for the longest time. It smelled like an old friend who wanted to embrace me and make the fear go away. It assured me that it would calm my frayed nerves. If I had this glass, just this one glass, I could relax and get some sleep. What harm would this one glass do? No one would know, it would be my secret. The bottle had been left over from a dinner party, it hadn't even cost us anything, I reasoned. I could smell the rich tannin wafting from the glass, and my mind was already tasting it. It would bring me comfort and get me through this night. What harm could it do?

It would do all the harm; it would do all the harm in the world! I picked up the glass and bottle. I needed to get rid of it. I needed to get it away from me, and fast. I moved into the kitchen and made directly for the sink. My heart lurched in tandem with the wine as it cascaded down the kitchen drain. The glug of the emptying rang in my ears. Placing the bottle on the edge of the counter, I stared at the sink, now stained a vibrant red. Part of me was questioning what I had just done. A pang of loss ran through me and the sight of those splashes hurt me. I needed them gone and away from me, I needed to get past this moment. I hurriedly grabbed the dishcloth and wiped the evidence away.

What use was I to anyone under the influence? What if the hospital called or one of the children needed me? 'Apologies, I was blowing off some steam, you're on your own.' Evidence removed, I took one last look at that empty sink, cross with myself for being so weak. This was not the type of person I wanted to be. I was better than this. I had to be better than this. My family deserved someone better than this.

I needed a clear mind and could not wallow in self-pity. I was being ridiculous, and when someone is being ridiculous, there is nothing more to be done except to remove that absurd person from the situation. I would deal with my weakness later, right now the only thing to do was to get out of my own way and try to sleep.

The surgery went well, thankfully, and he made a full recovery. The kids had the best time at my friend's place, to the point that she was given a spot on their list of favourite people. As for me, my friend from the pub was right. I did/do have a relationship with alcohol. I used it to blow off steam, to alleviate stress, celebrate and commiserate. It had invaded every part of my life. That night gave me a new respect for alcohol and the power that it can have. It was the crutch that I leaned on and I sometimes found myself limping without it.

There were other times over the year when I lamented not partaking. There's no point in saying that I was a fast learner, I'm not. However, as the year wore on it did get better, I missed it less and less. Ever so slowly, my relationship did change, being apart from something for that long does change the dynamic. It wasn't until late October, when we attended a fancy-dress Halloween party, that I noticed. Several hours into chatting with dead clowns, corpse brides, vampires and other such nightmare creatures I realised I had not thought about drinking. I was surrounded by good friends and conversation, living every minute of it. It was such a freeing feeling. Not having my crutch to lean on. It was a simple thing but significant to me. My relationship with alcohol had changed, and I liked it.

35

THE MANY BENEFITS OF A NO-ALCOHOL YEAR

After an entire twelve months of not drinking, I can vouch for the benefits of giving up alcohol. It has changed my life on many levels. It was challenging but also one of the best things that I've ever done for myself. There were so many benefits, some obvious, some not so obvious. I am going to start with the obvious one and take it from there.

THE BENEFITS

1. It Saves Money

Alcohol is expensive, particularly when added to the related costs of mixers, glasses, taxis, hotels stays, food, clothes, and goodness knows what else. These all add up to make drinking an expensive hobby to part take in.

2. Skin's Appearance Improved

Drinking alcohol is hard on the body, but it's especially hard on the skin. I don't think I fully realised the impact that even a small amount of alcohol can have. This was the first time I had gotten compliments on my skin in my whole life. Alcohol is a potent diuretic; it dehydrates the skin and reduces elasticity. The ruddiness in my complexion has dissipated, and some of the elasticity appears to have come back. Dark circles under my eyes have decreased noticeably. This has allowed my makeup and skincare products to stretch further.

3. Weight Loss

We all know this, but drinking puts on weight. In the first two months of the No-Spend Year, I lost 10 pounds. I had not planned to, and I didn't even notice until I realised that I was gone past the smallest hole on my belt. I cannot entirely attribute this to the alcohol, as part of it must have been due to banning takeaways and eating out. However, it was the first time in my life that I lost weight without even trying to, at a time in my life where I had no interest in losing weight.

4. Memory and Focus Have Improved

I have been, and always will be, a total scatterbrain. I don't think anything will ever change that trait. In saying that, over this year, my memory has improved. My ability to recall things and remember information has improved. It's almost like a fog has been lifted and that does feel good.

5. Health Improved

For the length of the No-Spend Year, I did not have a sniffle, cough or cold. I did not need to take any medicine, not so much as a throat lozenge. This is most definitely a first for me, and again, just like the weight loss, I believe that alcohol was part of the reason for this, along with a better diet due to the grocery budget and a small bit of exercise. Not having to buy medicines or go to a doctor has saved money too.

6. Sleeping Soundly

I sleep like a baby now. Alcohol lowers blood pressure and makes it harder for the body to get a good night's sleep. Even a small amount makes most people tired in the morning. Now that this barrier has been lifted, I am out like a light every night. A good night's sleep makes such a difference to the day. This has a direct impact on my kids' lives, as I'm better able to keep up with them. That feels fantastic.

7. The Relationship Gets Easier

In any good relationship, there's a balance. You're there for your friends, and they're there for you. I used to think that I needed alcohol for its lovely ability to be a social lubricant and make the conversation flow more easily. It took a while to get used to socialising without alcohol. Once I did adjust, things changed for the better. I began to own who I was and appreciate that I was acceptable company without a drink in hand. I learned that conversations weren't about me, they were about other people – a far more interesting topic. Chats became more enjoyable and immersive. I prefer the type of friend that I am now; I've learned more about the people around me this year than I ever knew before.

8. Mornings Are Mine Again

Not being slowed down by the effects of alcohol is a great feeling. I realised this year that I am a total early bird. I love getting up before 6 a.m. when the world is still asleep and easing into the day. My mind is clear, and I am doing things that I never considered doing before. One of those things is that I have developed a love of writing. Writing would not have been a forte of mine, ever, I would have always considered myself to be a Science and Maths person. Although my teachers would probably even question that aptitude! However, with the extra time that I have back from not drinking, I have been able to develop other skills, ones that I would not have had the confidence to even consider, let alone work on and improve.

9. I Feel I Am a Better Parent

One of the big reasons for committing to not drinking for the year was so I could be a good example to my kids. I have received far more from them in return for my one tiny sacrifice. I have more energy and time now. In the mornings, I am up before they are and get to kiss their sweaty foreheads as they wake. I am reading to them more at night, and our quality time together is better. I'm focused on them and on nothing else.

10. Control

Looking back, I can pinpoint times in my life when I let myself be led and just shuffled along with the crowd. I did shuffle along for various reasons: lack of confidence and energy but mainly because I didn't know what I wanted from life. So I went with what I thought I should wish for. Stepping back from alcohol for the year has given me a clearer head and more time to think and figure out what I want from life. I am making more decisions now based on what is best for my family and me and not what other people are doing. My actions are proactive and contribute to building a better, happier life, rather than the reactive one that I led before.

SUMMARY

I wasn't a big drinker when this all began. However, I am saying that with the caveat of being Irish. Drinking is part of our culture; it is a well-accepted pastime and is considered by many to be a hobby. Not having alcohol to slow me down allowed me to do more of the things that I love to do. It allows me to be a better friend, wife and mother. My relationship with alcohol has changed for the better because of the year. Even though I will not rule out drinking again, it will be with a different mindset – a more positive and in-control one.

36

THE ELECTRIC CAR

The electric car was the single most substantial financial risk we took all year. Making it our primary mode of transport drew one of the strongest reactions from our peers. Concerns about range, size and cost dominated conversations, despite my reassurances that due diligence had been done and my acknowledging that this was indeed a financial risk. Transitioning to an electric car as the primary source of transport had been on our radar, albeit not for several years, until technology advanced and they'd proven themselves as a reliable substitute for the traditional combustion engine car. However, a series of unfortunate events led us to shorten that time frame and take the leap earlier than planned.

Returning the company car when I stepped back from my job left us with a 10-year-old Estate with a 1.2 engine as our only car. My husband commuted to work on the motorbike. As long as I could do the school runs, grocery shop and the longer trips when required, we saw no need to upgrade. Cars had never been high on my social currency list, so we were content to stick with this machine for the foreseeable future.

Unfortunately, the car had other ideas. One month into our new life, I noticed oil drips all over the backyard. The garage diagnosed a leaking oil sump. Still sticking to the initial plan, we made the investment to fix it. However, brakes, drums, callipers, coils, a wing mirror, and several other items later, I wasn't feeling so generous anymore. We persisted, ever torn between sunk costs and the cost of getting a different car. Surely this expensive patch would come to an end soon?

It did, although not in the way we had anticipated. As I was returning from a school run one day, a painful sounding crunch came from the gearbox. All the gears went, except for first and third, and it was a hairy ride home. The afternoon was futilely spent ringing round scrap yards and dealerships, trying to find a new or second-hand gearbox at a reasonable price. It turned out that a 6-speed gearbox for this 10-year-old 1.2 Estate was right up there with Fabergé eggs in terms of both rarity and cost. We had to change the car, but the question was, to what type?

After much research and debate, we decided to take the leap and commit to a fully electric car. Whatever decision we made concerning the vehicle, it was going to be a significant outlay. The new plan was to go electric and keep it for at least ten to fifteen years.

THE REASONS FOR GOING ELECTRIC

1. Greater Reliability

As it is new and under warranty, it should take a long time before issues start to arise, compared with an older car. Too many days have been lost bringing a broken car to and from the garage. Had the car been a combustion engine car, we would have chosen a low mileage one that was a few years old. The premium attached to petrol or diesel is too high to buy new, in my opinion. However, the electric car came with favourable grants and a scrappage deal as well.

2. Lower Fuel Costs

Petrol and diesel are expensive line items in any budget. With an electric car, this budget item all but disappears. Changing electricity providers annually ensures that electricity stays affordable. We installed a NightSaver meter, which halved the cost of night-time charging, bringing the fuel cost even lower. Over the year this brought the charging cost down to approximately €1 per 100 km.

3. Lower Car Tax

Electric cars fall into the lowest tax bracket, saving money in that department, too. At the time of writing this, the lowest tax band is €120 per year.

4. Cheaper Servicing

An electric car is pretty much a laptop on wheels. Just like any laptop, it should be able to run for years with very little going wrong with it. Aside from tyres, brakes etc., there shouldn't be much to service. There are not as many moving parts to wear down as in a combustion engine. To date, the average servicing cost has been notably lower than with previous cars. Time will tell if this trend continues.

5. Convenient Refuelling at Home

There is a lovely convenience to having a full tank in the car every morning. No more hunting for a petrol station at 6 a.m. on a cold and frosty morning. Every morning the car has a full tank and is ready to go when you are.

6. Lower Carbon Footprint

Electric cars do not have emissions. I'm hoping that this will work in my favour too when it comes to the inevitable NCT in a few years.

7. Range

The electric car we bought has a maximum range of 290 km. Most of our driving is within 150 km of where we live. This almost eliminates the dependency on the external network for charging with the expectation for longer journeys. If a trip exceeds 200 km, I will at the very least need a coffee and the kids a run around, so a charging break is welcome. There is a whole array of apps to help plan trips according to where charge points are located, making planning trips much more manageable.

SUMMARY

One year in, driving an electric car has definitely been a game-changer from a running costs perspective. Based on my predictions, from approximately year four onwards, the electric car is easier on the pocket. The proof will be revealed over time, and much will depend on carbon taxes, government regulation, and fuel costs. While I understand that an electric car will not be suitable for everyone, it may be worth a second look to see if it might be a fit for your life and lifestyle.

PART VII

THE RESULTS

37

THE RESULTS

No alcohol, no new clothes or eating out, no takeaways or hair dye, minimalism embraced, and the whole mindful spending gambit optimised. Our whole world was turned upside down in the name of living within our means. Was it worth the effort? Did focusing on mindful spending have the impact it needed to be worth a year of our lives? Well, here are the numbers, judge for yourself.

For the purpose of ease, the mindful spending categories have been divided into six main areas:

1.   Groceries
2.   Discretionary
3.   Transport
4.   Childcare
5.   Household Bills
6.   Minimalism

1. GROCERIES

The budget was €100 per week to buy groceries, cleaning products, toiletries and for the general running of the house. The maximum for the year was €5,200. This meant that once we stayed below the €5,200 overall, the result was positive. In 2018 we spent €9,765.15 on groceries. The plan was to approximately halve that to care for the four of us and our two spoiled cats.

The total grocery spend for 2019 came in at €4,916.83, which was €283.17 (5.5 per cent) below the €5,200 budget. More significantly, this was

€4,848.32 less than the 2018 outlay, an almost 50 per cent reduction. The average spend per week in 2019 was €94.55. The average spend per week in 2018 was a notably higher €187.79. This one decision took massive pressure our finances. The goal of cutting our grocery budget in half was met, a goal that had been a pipe dream only a few months before.

The Christmas food shopping felt like the Christmases from my childhood. The sense of anticipation and excitement flooded back in a way that I never thought possible. A year of careful shopping and gathering small but consistent under-spends each week had created a nice extra cushion to enjoy over the festive season. At the beginning of December, we had spent only €4,327.95 of the total food budget. This left us with €872.05 for Christmas festivities.

The kids came with me to do the big Christmas shop. They each commandeered a small kid's trolley and loaded up with whatever they desired. They were in heaven, filling their carts with every treat that they could reach. It was the most fun day of shopping all year. In fact, it was one of the most fun days of the year. The excitement was palpable as they squealed their way around the aisles. At one stage, my daughter declared that she would be happy to do another No-Spend Year if it meant that she could treat herself like this again at Christmas. You could have knocked me over with a feather. Even with our relaxed spending over those last few weeks, we managed to remain within budget.

When I look back at how we ate before this year began, there have been some significant changes in our habits. I had assumed that we ate well before this. However, in comparison, now we eat notably less processed food and red meat. We not only ate more fruit and vegetables but bought more sustainably farmed, fair-trade, free-range and organic food than when we spent double the amount on food. We have also managed to keep many of our preferred brands, too. It was a balance between reducing food waste and being conscious of what we bought.

One observation – it may be a coincidence, or maybe it was our improved diets mixed with an outdoor lifestyle; whatever the case, I think it is worth mentioning. For the whole year, there was not a sniffle, cough or cold in the house, which was most definitely a first for us. Without fail, every other year my son has had croup, landing him in the emergency room on more than one occasion. All of us would at some stage suffer from a cold, virus or chest infection. This year was the exception and our medicine cabinet is one of the least used corners of our home now; it contains little more than a few plasters, antiseptic ointment and paracetamol. Medicine is typically a full line item in the budget, but not this year. Less money was spent on health, doctor's visits and medicines. By my reckoning, there was probably close to an additional €500 saved in this regard alone.

The Weekly Grocery Numbers

Here are the final numbers for the food budget, broken down into their respective weeks. Some weeks were better than others, but in the end, it all worked out.

Week	Amount
Week 1	€99.87
Week 2	€110.40
Week 3	€80.99
Week 4	€69.91
Week 5	€101.55
Week 6	€55.08
Week 7	€94.55
Week8	€72.90
Week 9	€93.28
Week 10	€96.28
Week 11	€80.43
Week 12	€71.52
Week 13	€95.80
Week 14	€71.67
Week 15	€90.80
Week 16	€96.09
Week 17	€86.61
Week 18	€92.43
Week 19	€96.98
Week 20	€107.05
Week21	€89.32
Week22	€95.98
Week 23	€102.15
Week 24	€99.99
Week 25	€98.54
Week 26	€100.00
Week 27	€68.79
Week 28	€96.72
Week 29	€72.00
Week 30	€95.76
Week 31	€84.99
Week 32	€91.80
Week 33	€92.16
Week 34	€91.03
Week 35	€69.84
Week 36	€96.76
Week 37	€98.46
Week 38	€93.94
Week 39	€99.54
Week 40	€106.80
Week 41	€72.02
Week 42	€99.51
Week 43	€85.91
Week 44	€100.16
Week45	€93.91
Week 46	€91.15
Week 47	€92.01
Week 48	€84.52
Week 49	€97.04
Week 50	€147.36
Week 51	€152.94
Week 52	€191.54
	€4,916.83

Grocery Cost reduction versus 2018: €4,848.32, or a 50 per cent drop

2. DISCRETIONARY SPEND

Our 2019 discretionary spend totalled €8,266.69. This worked out as an average of €688.89 per month, or €158.97 per week. In 2018 the numbers were significantly different: €15,349.93 for the year, or €1,279.16 per month, which is €295.19 per week. We managed to reduce our total discretionary spending by €7,083.24, which is a drop of over 46 per cent – 6 per cent more than was aimed for.

When it came to discretionary spending, things like holidays, days out, vet bills, kids' clothes, school fees, swimming lessons, dental visits and any family spends that were not an essential bill or grocery-related all came under this category. This did include the new dishwasher and oil tank, both unexpected expenses, but these things happen and are part of living.

Family Holiday

We chose to have the same holiday in the same accommodation for both 2018 and 2019. The total spend came to €602 in 2019, compared to €1,257 in 2018. The same holiday cost less than half what it had the previous year, and not one of us noticed any difference except in our pockets. The kids had fun and spent the entire time either in wet suits or sturdy trainers.

Focusing on outdoor activities like hiking, swimming and visiting parks with picnics, instead of eating out and having take-away coffees and nights in pubs made all the difference.

No-Spend Days

These were a critical habit that allowed this year to happen. It did take some getting used to, but No-Spend Days proved to be one of the best things that we've ever invested in. Our local library became a gold mine of free workshops, talks and group meetings, along with the traditional wealth of books, magazines, DVDs and games. The kids learned to weave, felt, knit, and the summer reading competition kept them busy for the rainier days. We explored many of the free parks, castles, hikes and trails to be found around Ireland, always bringing our camper stove for impromptu cooked-up picnics. In autumn we spent days gathering berries, seeds and nuts for jams, roasting and chutneys.

Over the year we had 231 No-Spend Days out of 365. I have no idea what it would have been in previous years, although it is safe to assume that the number was significantly lower, knowing my older, loose spending habits.

Discretionary Cost reduction versus 2018: €7,083.24, a drop of over 46 per cent.

3. TRANSPORT

Transitioning from a two-car, two motorbike household to having one commuter motorbike and one electric car was a significant risk. The bike continues to work well as a commuter bike. Even though we are only one year into having the electric car, it is holding its own from a financial perspective. The servicing cost, road tax and tolls are massively reduced. The electricity, if charged at home, worked out as €1 per 100 km. The cost of insurance has also dropped with the EV compared to my previous, older 2008 car. I had assumed that moving from an older car with third-party fire and theft insurance to a new, fully comprehensive electric one would have brought up the premium, but not so.

All these savings combined more than cancelled out the financing we took to get the car, making it almost cost-neutral. We plan to keep it for the next ten years or more.

Transportation reduction versus 2018: €3,929.91.

4. CHILDCARE

Having two young children in childcare was a necessary but significant drain on our finances over the last decade. At one stage we were paying close to €2,000 per month, or €24,000 per year, to have the kids cared for. Thankfully as they got older this did lessen to a more manageable €10,700 per year. As grateful as we were for the excellent care that they got over the years, it was still a princely sum to be parting with for the privilege of going to work. Once I stepped back, this was an immediate reduction in our outgoings.

Household bill reduction versus 2018: €10,700, or a 100 per cent drop.

5. HOUSEHOLD BILL REDUCTION

As each utility bill came up for renewal, every effort was made to shop around and get the best price and service available at the time. For the most part, changing provider was straightforward and rarely took more than a few minutes per switch.

Once the home charger was installed for the car, I did change to a NightSaver meter, which allowed for cheaper rates for night-time electricity use. I hadn't realised until this year that most of the appliances, like the dishwasher and washing machine, had timers built into them. These came in very handy for taking advantage of the new pricing structure.

Household bill reduction versus 2018: €901

6. MINIMALISM

Embracing minimalism had a positive impact on our home. Half-filled boxes have been emptied and cupboards reclaimed. It feels like our home can breathe again. Everything now has a function and makes our lives better for being there. The house can still be messy at times, but it is easier to maintain, and my cleaning schedule is less demanding. Our home evolved from an overstuffed storage unit to a functional, warm, organised and lived-in nest. It is not perfect, but I don't waste time every day searching for stray items or buying extra things because I have misplaced them. This works well for us as a family.

Buying habits changed with the advent of minimalism. Mindful spending became the norm. Rarely does anything come into the house now unless it has a legitimate purpose. Knowing there are fewer plastic toys around feels good. The kids warmed well to their pocket money regime. They enjoy the sense of satisfaction that comes with buying something that they have earned.

Even though minimalism did not directly save money, what it did do was lessen the need to spend more. With fewer things to maintain, care for and store away, less money is spent on cleaning products, repairing and storage. What it did was to negate the need for extra storage. I thought we would require more before the project began but it turns out we just needed less stuff.

THE FINAL NUMBERS

Metrics	2018	2019
Groceries	€9,765.15	€4,916.83
Discretionary	€15,349.93	€8,266.69
Petrol	€5,542.94	€1,362.53
Electricity for electric car	N/A	€250.50
Childcare	€10,700	N/A
No-Spend Days	N/A	231 of 365
Total year expenses	€41,358.02	€14,796.55
Expenses difference		€26,561.47
Total household bill reduction		+€901
Total expense reduction 2018 vs 2019		€27,462.47

SUMMARY

For 2019, as a family we reduced our outgoings by €27,462.47. This is all post-tax money, so the real amount as a gross salary is a massive number. Somewhere in the region of €37- €40,000, I believe. When it came to totting up the results at the end of the year, I was quite nervous. I put my family through twelve months of rules and worried that if there wasn't a significant difference to our finances, then I had put them through it for nothing. I had thought several times during the year that maybe it wouldn't work and that it was time to admit defeat and spend the rest of my life apologising profusely to them for my ill-thought-out the experiment.

I knew that there would be savings this year, but I did not for a moment think that the numbers would come out so strong. I worried that I was putting my family's financial future in jeopardy. Instead, I have learned that with a little planning and consistently doing the small things well, significant economic changes can be made.

RESULTS MINDSET

It is done. 365 days of mindful spending completed transformed our lives. This year has changed how we live, how we see the world and how I see myself. In January of every year, without fail, I was that person who would vow to become better, eat well or get fit. I would spend hundreds of euro on juicers, gadgets or whatever the latest self-improvement fad was. Like clockwork, I failed every time, and I failed hard. Each year all I had to show for my bucket of best intentions was a bruised bank balance and an ever-increasing sense of failure.

I thought that if I wore the right clothes, liked the right things or went to the right places, I would figure out what this secret was and get ahead like everyone else. I thought that if I drove the right car and bought the right books, I could carve out an acceptable niche for myself and have status among my peers. I spent so long doing what I thought I should be doing and following the dreams that I should be following that I forgot entirely what I even wanted for myself or my life. This year held the mirror up and made me realise that I am a lot more than the things I own. I did not lose my mind – I found my mind, a mind that I had bypassed to follow the 'shoulds' for far too long.

Applying the habits of mindful spending during the No-Spend Year gave me the right practices to make the best of our single income. The No-Spend Year forced me to distance myself from the material world. It made me wash all the glitter away and take a good hard look at what I was made of. I peeled back the ego, the pride and self-interest, cutting out chunks of insecurity and low self-worth, after layers of pulling, tearing, stripping and sanding. I began to see a new version of myself. I began to see a person I didn't recognise at first. I began to see a plainer, simpler person. I saw a person who was interested in the world around her who enjoyed the people in it. This person was kinder and more real than ever before. This was a person who sought people out for the joy and company and drew pleasure from the simpler things in life. This person was happy.

Harnessing the power of mindful spending was the key to achieving this. Paring back the wants was how I kick-started balancing out the negative financial hole where my salary had once been. For this to happen, I had to evolve away from my old habits and create new, better practices in their place. I changed the way things had been done in times past and embraced a whole new way of living. It took grit every day to stay on track. However, the small, assured changes slowly accumulated, all those little steps practised over and over again allowed us to achieve over €27,000 in household reductions. These habits not only produced remarkable financial results, but they will enable me to live a free life that I love.

Part VIII

PULLING IT ALL TOGETHER

38

CONCLUSION

Before mindful spending became a part of my life, I let myself be told what I wanted to be, what I should say, think and aim for. I thought the world knew some secret and was refusing to share. I was staring at a universe that seemed to have it all together while I held on with my fingertips.

Fear prevented me from seeing a clear path. It took the longest time to figure out the first step. When I did figure it out, I still had no idea what the second step would look like. I just knew that this had to be the first one. My children were growing up so fast, and I wanted more than anything to be at home more often. Time was not on my side, I had to choose.

The path I chose may not be for you, or maybe it is – or, more likely, a version of it is. Only you can decide that. However, what I do know is that we only have one shot at this life, and it is only us, ourselves, on our own, who have to live our lives. We cannot live it for convention or for what we think we should be doing. We need to live our lives for ourselves and our loved ones. If you find that, you find happiness.

Developing the mindful spending habits and applying them to a No-Spend Year has taught me so much about living. I know I have peace of mind if there is a job loss – we can handle it – and if there is uncertainty, we can handle that, too. The foundations are laid. They are strong foundations, strong enough to build a life of our design. Now the fun really begins.

I have changed my perspective on so many things. I used to think nothing of frittering away money on regular takeaways or clothing sales. Now I see that same money in a different light and value it for what it is. It is the tangible evidence of time, education and experience traded for cash. I have learned to respect that time and effort, by slowing down and thinking about how that time and energy are spent. I make it work as hard for us as we worked to earn it in the first place.

SMALL CHANGES HAVE A BIG IMPACT

I have learned that small, seemingly insignificant actions over time yield worthy results. Big gestures don't always have the same effect, they take much effort and are hard to repeat. Small, consistent habits over time led to reducing our outgoings by over €27,000, so much more than I could ever have imagined. So when it comes to frittering small amounts of money, just remember this ...

To save €10,000 in a year, all you need to do is stop mindlessly spending €27.40 per day.

Once I started looking at money from a place of respect and value, spending choices became a very different animal. Unnecessary items purchased became burdens and drains on my resources. These net worth vampires sucked the rewards of our life's work out of us and stole from our future. This is real deprivation. On the other hand, putting money into a pension, paying down my mortgage or growing a Rainy-Day Fund, that is freedom, that is choice. That is self-care.

This year taught me the importance of quality. Value is more than just monetary. Before this year, I would have scoured the lower end of the market as my way of saving money. I know now that, for the most part, this was a false economy. I sometimes compromised on the quality of clothes and electrical and other goods if I could get a better price. These things did not last; they were not as durable as I needed them to be. I realised I needed fewer things but those things needed to be of better quality.

For all the money spent on cheap, fast fashion that was removed from my wardrobe this year, I could have created a smaller, fantastic, high-quality wardrobe for the same price. It would have saved me time and energy and I would have felt better in myself. This rise in quality was also reflected in our food. With only half the budget we are eating better, more sustainably and with less waste than we ever did on twice the budget. The focus shifted from the mindless filling of the trolley to waste reduction. From now on, I have adopted a 'less but better' mentality and am mindful of my choices.

My relationship with money and the value that it can bring was not the only relationship to change. My relationship with alcohol changed, too. I did have a relationship with it, and a strong one at that. Distancing myself from drinking for so long has given me to time to evaluate where it fits into my life. I do not want it or enjoy it the way I used to, I have lost the taste for it – for the most part, at least. I don't see it as having any really beneficial role in my life anymore. I do not need it as a crutch or as the social lubricant that I thought it was. Alcohol is not bad in itself; however, the relationship is different now we are not as close as we once were. I am perfectly fine keeping it as a good acquaintance and not the close friend and confidante that it once was.

Embracing minimalism has had a lasting impact too. I remember flicking through magazines and online sites displaying aspirational homes with bright, airy rooms and muted, elegant colour schemes. I've coveted the voile window drapes and pure white, smudge-free walls. In the past, I would think how lovely it would be just to click my fingers and have this idyllic image appear right here in my own home. The truth was that when I cleared out all those extra belongings. I did not know what I liked. I hadn't slowed down before to figure that out.

I know now that I do not want a perfect home, nor do I want a labyrinth of clutter. I want it to be my family home, which is open, clean and comfortable. It took a long time to figure that out. Now I know what I want our home to be like. I also know how I want our house to feel. It does not have to appeal to anyone else, only us, and that is a freeing sensation.

It also means less cleaning, dusting, minding, servicing, insuring, storing, manoeuvring and organising. This gives me more time to do what I want with my life. My version of minimalism, while not by the book, allows me to focus more energy on building the best experience that I can for my family.

We All Have Different Paths to Walk

Being there for my kids now when they come home from school means everything to me. It makes me happy. Figuring that out was the key to pretty much everything. Stepping back as I did would be a bit left field for most. However, what I want you to take away from this is to value the money that you work so hard to earn. In turn, make that money work as hard for you as you do for it.

Each person's path is different. The journey of life is never a straight line, for most of us it is a series of zigs and zags and loops and knots, but if you can figure out what it is that will make you happy in life, all you need to do then is apply the powerful habits of mindful spending, allowing each decision you make to bring you closer to your perfect life.

So whatever it is that you value above all else, figure it out and funnel all your time, energy and money into that one life that beats all the rest. The one that leaves you sitting in your rocking chair, 120 years of age, smiling that secret smile to yourself – the smile that only a truly contented, satisfied and happy person has.

Mindful spending is the ultimate act of self-care and self-love. It is also one of the best philosophies to improve not only your life but the lives of those around you. A happier, healthier, more secure version of you will emerge and will give you the energy and will to help others.

Be the change.

39

HOW CAN THIS CHALLENGE CHANGE YOUR LIFE?

Maybe you think what I did was a fantastic and life-changing idea, or perhaps you think it was extreme. Wherever this book sits in your mind, here's some guidance that you can apply to your life to get you started on your money journey.

FIND YOUR VALUES

Figure out what is important to you in life – trust me, this will be time well spent. Whether it is extra time with the kids, travel, learning new things or simply being the best at what you do, understanding your driving force will help you find that happy sweet spot in life. Once you know what those values are, any decisions from that point onwards should be measured against those values. If a decision brings you closer to those values, then go for it. If it takes you away from them, walk away.

SET GOALS

Now that you have figured out your values, the things that make you happy in life, the next step is to work out your goals. Goals are missions that have tangible endpoints. For example, a value might be that you love music and can't live without it in your life because it makes you truly happy. A goal might be to go to a particular festival six months from now and to do that you need to save €50 per month to pay for the ticket, travel, accommodation and incidentals. It is going to be very obvious if you hit that goal or not. Setting goals gives you the steps to achieve anything you want.

KNOW WHERE YOU ARE

Calculating your net worth is an excellent way to see what your starting point is. If you know where you are, then it is easier to make the journey to where you want to be. To calculate your net worth, add up all your assets (car, home, savings, pension, etc.) and take away your liabilities (mortgage, loans, debt, etc.). For some of you, it may make for grim reading and cause a bit of a shock to the system. However, for others, you might get a pleasant surprise and find you are in a better financial situation than you thought. Either way, it is essential to know. Take the time to figure this out.

DRAW UP THAT CASHFLOW

A cashflow in its simplest form is a way to tell your money where to go. Having one that works for you and is tailored to your life can be a magical thing. A good cashflow gives each euro that you work so hard to earn a job to do and a place to be. It is excellent for curbing unnecessary spending and building up that net worth.

UNDERSTAND YOUR EMOTIONAL TRIGGERS

Money can be a very emotional thing, and all of us have deep-rooted money stories that we carry within us. Spend some time watching how and when you spend money. Notice the times when you are spending to make yourself feel better or because you are tired. Try to pull back on opening your wallet at these times or remove yourself from those situations, if possible. These are substantial money drains that do nothing to move your life forward.

TRY A NO-SPEND DAY

A No-Spend Day is a day where no money is spent except on essential bills or from the grocery budget. These are days when takeaways, coffees, impulse clothes purchases and other frivolous spending are off the table. Focus instead on things that do not cost money. Things like free events, visiting friends, time in parks, the countryside or, my favourite, the local library. There are so many fun things to do that do not cost money. Give it a try, I dare you.

TRY A SHOPPING BAN

We all have our weaknesses, be it online shopping, clothes sales, cute fluffy cushions or jazzy new stationary. Start with one thing, like not buying new clothes for a month, or soft furnishings, or even candles. If you find this too easy, then stretch yourself with an all-out shopping ban for a month or, like me, a year.

USE MINDFULLY

Another way to reduce spending is to do a use-up challenge. This is a great way to focus on what you already have before you buy any more. Pick an item or area in your life like beauty products, makeup or perfume. Use up whatever it is entirely before you purchase more. You might be surprised at how much you have stored away already in the recesses of those cupboards.

EMBRACE MINIMALISM

There are so many things in the world that promise all sorts of life-changing results – gadgets, trinkets, products. It can be overwhelming at times. Figure out what material possessions you need to keep that make your life more comfortable or make it work better. Move anything that does not bring value or make you happy out of your life. When it comes to purchasing new things, take the time to think about why you are buying it and what purpose it will fulfil.

UNDERSTAND THE POWER OF SMALL CHANGES

Getting to grips with spending is not usually accomplished in one big grand gesture, it is the accumulation of small changes made consistently over time. Putting a value on the little spends and being more mindful in purchasing choices goes very far when it comes to saving money. Don't underestimate the power you have right at your fingertips every day.

Doing some or all of these things will make a positive impact on your finances, how deep you go down the rabbit hole is up to you. Taking control of your money and telling it where to go is not only empowering, it also removes stress from your life and allows you to focus on the things that really make you happy.

EPILOGUE

When New Year's evening came, I was not watching the clock willing the night away. I was not racing to the end, wishing for midnight. I was enjoying another evening with my friends. I did not miss alcohol or scroll the websites looking for what to buy in the sales. Quite the opposite, I did not want the evening to end. I was happy to chat, play cards and spend that time with my friends.

The next morning I woke up to my new rules-free world, life had permission to continue. I had the freedom to choose whatever I wanted again. Interestingly, very little changed; I preferred to keep many of my new habits. I have not dyed my hair. The food budget stayed in place. Takeaways and eating out are a seldom but much-anticipated experience now. I appreciate the ceremony of getting dressed up and going out for a meal – keeping it as a rare treat makes it unique and exciting. I do not want to tip back into my old habits again and lose the excitement of a special night out with friends and food.

Sustainable bamboo socks were the prized item with which I officially broke the shopping fast. I have a new appreciation for owning fewer things and derive great pleasure from each of them. I still treasure and am grateful for this precious time with my children. Just like my children, I hope I will never take my friends and possessions for granted. Happiness resides in the details; it's the small things that make the difference in our lives. People and how we are with them, that's what makes life rich and happy. Whether it's your finances or your happiness, you have to choose to nurture them if you want them to blossom.

The No-Spend Year of 2019 has changed my life at a fundamental level. I can say with certainty that it was the best thing that I have ever done for my family or myself. This year has changed our finances and work–life balance. More importantly, our health and our quality of life have improved because of it. I honestly thought back in January that I wouldn't make it past the first month, let alone a whole year. Yet here I stand, a happier, healthier, financially stronger version of myself.

So much about my life has changed: who I am and the type of person I want to be. Every day we make choices. These choices show us who we are and what we want to be, but that's the fun of being alive. It's the fantastic thing about being human.

Once we know our values, we can align our life and life choices with them, using the habits of mindful spending. That is one great truth in life.

I have discovered a second great truth in life. That second truth is:

I am enough.

You are enough.

We are enough.

APPENDIX

SMART MONEY GUIDES

HOW TO SURVIVE
THE WEEKLY GROCERY SHOP

1. MAKE A LIST

Check the cupboards, fridge and freezer to see what you have to work with and meal-plan with what is already there. Chances are, many of the items you need are already lurking on your shelves. Only put the things and amounts required on the list. Take the guesswork out of this. Check the recipe for specifics if you're in doubt.

2. BRING THE LIST

I can't count the number of times I have painstakingly made a list only to leave it on the kitchen counter. It is the map to guide you.

3. BRING SHOPPING BAGS

Don't waste your precious budgetary resources; keep a supply of shopping bags, trolley tokens and anything else you need in the same place in your kitchen – in plain sight is ideal for helping to jog the memory. I also always bring reusable produce bags. They are great for reducing waste and extra packaging and make it easier to buy loose items.

4. BE A LONE RANGER

If possible, go grocery shopping alone. The fewer 'helpers' you have, the better. Fewer opinions, fewer distractions, more focus. Going alone may mean shopping later or earlier in the day than usual, but it will be worth it.

5. Keep the Entourage's Energy Levels Up

If shopping alone is not an option, bring water and snacks for the trip. Having homemade options on hand will help prevent unwanted purchases from sneaking into the trolley.

6. Fuel Up Before You Begin

Don't go shopping on an empty stomach. You are only human, and stores are designed to help you part with your money. Don't add extra temptation just because you forgot to have breakfast.

7. Bring Only the Money that You Need

Bring only the amount of cash with you that you have to spend on groceries and stick to it. If you tend to use a card, more discipline may be required here. Limiting cash is a hard one to stick to, but it will curb the purchasing of unnecessary impulse items.

8. Stick to the List

Your list is your rule book. Resist temptations, do not deviate. You will regret it later. As cute as that extra plush cushion looks now, it does not constitute a meal and neither does that extra-large bag of crisps on promotion. If it is not on the list, it does not get bought.

9. Promotions Are Missable

If you see an item on promotion and it is not on your list, leave it there. Special offers happen every day of the week. Remember it is not a one-time-only offer, and no, it is not unmissable.

10. Skirt the Edges of the Store

Stay away from centre aisles. The staples that you need tend to be at the edges of the shop. Store layouts encourage you to work through them aisle by aisle. If you have to go by the centre aisles, feel free to close your eyes as you hurry past.

11. Be Wary of Coupons

These are the red herrings of the shopping world. I am not a fan of coupons, simply since most of them are for items that aren't regular purchases. Many also seem to be for processed items that already have a premium on them and are not on the shopping list in the first place. If you have a coupon that gives money off your entire shop and you know beforehand that you will reach that threshold, by all means, go ahead. Otherwise, use coupons seldom and wisely.

12. Go Generic (Sort Of)

Be selective about the brand name products that you buy. Compare the generic to the branded item for ingredients and price. If the branded product can justify its price, then go for it, and enjoy it. There will be items that you love to have, that bring the value they promise. However, if you cannot find a significant taste, flavour, or ethical difference between the two, then go with the one that is kinder on the pocket.

13. Avoid Lazy Food

Prepacked and prepared food is usually more expensive and has extra colourings, flavourings, preservatives, salt or sugar added. Try to buy food in as natural a form as possible. It will not only save you money, it will be better for your health in the long run.

14. Check All the Levels on the Shelves

We can be lazy. Supermarkets know this. Premium products live at eye-level, with cheaper items on the upper and lower shelves. Search the higher and lower shelves for the best prices. Always check the price per kilogram, because things like nuts and dried fruit found in the baking aisles are often cheaper per kilogram than their snack aisle counterparts.

15. Prepare a Return Feast

Think ahead and plan an easy supper for that evening. Many of us are guilty of getting the shopping and then ordering a take-away that night because we are too 'tired' to cook. Put a chicken in the oven before you go or buy a pre-roasted one while you're out. Being prepared means there is something quick to eat as soon as we get home.

16. KNOW YOUR BLIND SPOTS

If time is of the essence or you know that temptation may strike, order online and have it delivered. It might cost a little to get it delivered, but it will save you time, money and impulse buys.

17. BONUS TIP: SHOP AROUND

Share the wealth, spread your weekly shopping across several stores to get the best overall prices; local suppliers can do great deals if you do your research. Many shops now have apps that can help you see what is on special that week. Know the offers in each store before you leave the house and keep to your list.

HOW TO FIND YOUR PERFECT FOOD BUDGET NUMBER

Have you have ever tried to make a food budget and found yourself continually failing, not sticking to the plan, getting frustrated and just giving up? Well, not anymore. Things are going to change around here. So stop beating yourself up, dust yourself off and read on.

Let's start with some home truths. It's not you – and it's not me either, by the way. Food is just one of those funny things that can get out of control if it's not managed correctly. You could spend your entire salary on food alone and be able to justify every purchase.

For a food budget to work, it has to allow you and your family to eat well while not wasting food. There is little point in picking an arbitrarily low number and depriving yourself. That is unsustainable and will most likely have you pulling our hair out and giving up. Decades of failed New Year's resolutions have shown us this by now.

The system that I am going to teach you will change how you approach food shopping and help you develop a different mindset entirely. A mindset that focuses on what you have, what's available at a reasonable price and what you like to eat. This tool will help you not only to get grocery spending under control but will reduce food waste and make sure that you are getting value for money.

The first and foremost thing to remember is that a food budget needs to be personal to you and your family's needs. Picking an arbitrary number or trying to mirror what other people are doing will not work. Every family is at a different stage in life, and every family has different needs. Stop comparing what you eat with what other people consume.

Here is an easy way to figure out what your sustainable food budget number is and how to stick to it. Follow these steps and make a difference to your pocket, health and the environment.

Step 1: Track How Much You Are Currently Spending

To know where you are going, you need to know where you are. Take a few weeks to understand how much you are spending, where you shop and what you buy. This will give you a benchmark to start from.

Step 2: Decrease Your Current Food Spend by 10 Per Cent

Let's just say you spend €150 on average per week on groceries. Set yourself a maximum target of €135. That is a reduction of €15. Work on staying at this level for several weeks until it becomes your routine. This 10 per cent reduction alone will give you back a massive €780 in savings over the year.

Step 3: Reduce Waste

Look at the items that end up in the bin or going to waste. It might be a carrot here or a banana there. These foods entered your home in perfectly good condition. Try to figure out why they never got eaten. These are the items that need to be tackled first. Either stop buying them or find better ways of storing or freezing them before they end up in the bin. Prioritise this food in the following week's dishes. Every piece of food saved is money in your pocket. Buying already frozen food may be an option here.

Step 4: Use Your Freezer Correctly

If your freezer is overflowing with random leftovers from five years ago then maybe it is time for a clear-out. Start using the items that are stored in your freezer. There's often a lot of money's worth of food tied up in there. Unfreeze and defrost those assets and put them to work. Check your freezer before each shop to prevent overbuying.

Step 5: Before Each Shop Stock Check

Do a stock check of your fridge, freezer and cupboards before you head out. See what is already opened and needs to be used up; these items should be the basis of your next few meals. This will curb spending on unnecessary things and reduce waste.

STEP 6: REPEAT

Repeat steps 2–5 until you have reduced your food budget to a manageable and reasonable level. You will know that you have reached that perfect level when you can comfortably eat well for the week while creating minimal food waste.

BONUS STEP

Put the money saved from the grocery budget towards debt, a Rainy-Day Fund or into other savings. This will, over time, have a true impact on your net worth. Most real wealth is built slowly over time.

TIPS FOR FAMILY HOLIDAYS IN IRELAND

You may love your home, but a change of scenery now and again is good for the soul. From my experience, the soul is at its happiest when it can relax and enjoy the downtime consequence-free. This includes not blowing the budget and putting yourself under massive financial strain for the sake of a few days off the clock.

Here are my tips on how to have a family holiday to remember while still keeping within the budget.

1. Go for Self-Catering

Ireland has such a fantastic range of rentals, self-catering and holiday home options. If it is for a few days or several weeks, this is a cost-effective way to get a place to stay. Hiring an apartment, camper van or house will give you plenty of space to relax and the freedom to do what you want when you want, be that cooking or eating out or in – self-catering gives you that flexibility. Quality accommodation makes it easy to put down roots for the length of your stay. Many self-catering places have BBQs and areas to relax outside. In the evenings you can play your choice of music and enjoy some much-needed chill-out time while the young ones sleep safe and sound nearby.

Self-catering doesn't have to be strictly so; there are many B&Bs that give flexibility to families and hotels often have on-site houses for holiday renting, with the benefit of providing access to the pool and other amenities. There is something out there for everyone.

2. Location, Location, Location

Location is one of the fundamental aspects of a great holiday in Ireland. We are so lucky in this country. It is built for adventure and experiences for all levels of ability. Every parent knows that entertaining the little ones is vital. That said, it is essential to have a holiday and not just a few expensive days away. Whether it is by the beach or near the mountains, lakes or rivers, pick a location with natural attractions that you can enjoy without hassle, travel or expense.

3. Bring Your Company with You

This one can make all the difference. Where young children are involved, it can be challenging to have a social life without needing babysitters. Extra minding adds more costs to an already expensive endeavour. Ask friends who have children of a similar age if they want to join you on holiday. A request like this may seem like a daunting idea at first, but once you consider the support that comes with having such company, it might seem like a better option.

a.   The kids are company for each other.
b.   When a parent is at the same point in life as their friend, activities and pastimes will overlap.
c.   There is no need to spend the entire holiday together, separate family days out are manageable, or if a couple wants to have a date night, the other couple can babysit.
d.   Many of the costs can be shared equally between both families, which helps to keep the outlay under control.

4. Activities

Days out do not have to be eye-wateringly expensive. Most days don't have to cost anything at all. Check out the local area for outdoor public play parks, walks, and hikes. Ireland is fortunate to have a rich history, with many old houses and demesnes. Many of these are free or have a nominal fee. Being close to a beach, lake or river is also a winner.

During the summers there are plenty of festivals on and many of these have free activities and events; all you have to do is turn up. Check out the local tourist office and library when you arrive in the area for more ideas.

5. Eating In

Contrary to popular opinion, it is not against the law to eat in while on holiday, nor do meals have to be complicated. The country is awash with supermarkets, country stores and local suppliers where you can pick up pizzas, fresh crispy bread and easy, tasty things that take your fancy. We have great local produce too that can be bought and cooked simply and quickly.

A little portable camping stove and frying pan are worth their weight in gold, too. Suppose you are heading out for the day and don't feel like cold sandwiches. Just grab a camping stove, a few sausages and head out. Eating outdoors is such a fun way to eat; the kids will love it.

6. Eating Out

Many parents find the combination of restaurants and children a risky business at times. Eating out should be a luxury treat as opposed to a daily routine. Eat out sparingly, earlier in the day and at well-chosen eateries. Thoroughly enjoy the experience when you do – make it an occasion as well as a satiating meal.

7. Be Prepared for All Weathers

Let's face it; it's Ireland. We have a fantastic green, lush countryside bursting with life and health. However, to enjoy this lush green land of ours, we have to accept the inevitable rain. We cannot change the weather, but we can change how we relate to it. Bring a waterproof windbreaker and boots and invest in a wetsuit. A proper wetsuit does not only guarantee a good day out at the beach, it is handy at home too. Sticking one on the kids and sending them out into the back garden on those rainy summer afternoons will keep them happy and warm for ages. If you have a trampoline, you are onto a winner.

8. Bring a Deck of Cards

It doesn't matter where you are from or what age you are, a deck of cards is universal. It can be an impromptu game of Snap with the kids on the beach or an evening of poker with your friends. A deck of cards is small, portable and majorly versatile, there are so many games to be played with them.

A holiday should be relaxing and fun. It is about new experiences and spending time with loved ones. Holidays are for making memories and laughing out loud. They are not about how much cash you can blow through or about stressing about how you will pay it back. Focus instead on what you value and what you consider a good time. What should stand out are memories and laughs, rather than souvenirs and maxed-out credit cards.

ENDNOTES

[1] McCarthy, F.D. (1992) '"Ireland's Economy in the 1980s: Stagnation and Recovery": A Comment', *Economic & Social Review*, available from: http://www.tara.tcd.ie/handle/2262/66541.

[2] Central Statistics Office, *Financial Interest Rates (Historical Series) by Interest Rate and Month*, StatBank, available from: https://statbank.cso.ie/px/pxeirestat/Statire/SelectVarVal/saveselections.asp.

[3] Alvarez, L. (2005) 'Suddenly Rich, Poor Old Ireland Seems Bewildered', *New York Times*, 2 February, available from: https://www.nytimes.com/2005/02/02/world/europe/suddenly-rich-poor-old-ireland-seems-bewildered.html.

[4] Fitz Gerald, J. (1999) 'Understanding Ireland's Economic Success', ESRI Working Paper No. 111.

[5] Bambrick, L. (2019) 'The Marriage Bar : A Ban on Employing Married Women', *Irish Congress of Trade Unions*, 14 October, available from: https://www.ictu.ie/blog/2019/10/14/the-marriage-bar-a-ban-on-employing-married-women/.

[6] FitzGerald, G. (2007) 'What Caused the Celtic Tiger Phenomenon?', *Irish Times*, 21 July, available from: https://www.irishtimes.com/opinion/what-caused-the-celtic-tiger-phenomenon-1.950806.

[7] Oireachas Library & Research Service (2007) 'The Housing Market in Ireland: Interest Rates, Credit Regulation and Subprime Lending', *Spotlight No. 2*, available from: https://data.oireachtas.ie/ie/oireachtas/libraryResearch/2007/2007-05-31_spotlight-the-housing-market-in-ireland_en.pdf

[8] Peet, J. (2004) 'The Luck of the Irish', *The Economist*, 16 October, available from: https://www.economist.com/special-report/2004/10/16/the-luck-of-the-irish.

[9] Elliott, L. (2009) 'Mr Austerity Tending Celtic Tiger's Wounds', *The Guardian*, 28 May, available from: https://www.theguardian.com/business/2009/may/28/irish-finance-minister-profile.

[10] BBC (2012) 'Northern Rock Run "Preventable"', *BBC News*, 13 June, available from: https://www.bbc.com/news/business-18419434.

[11] *NAMA*, available from: https://www.nama.ie/.

12 European Commission, Directorate-General for Economic and Financial Affairs (2011) *The Economic Adjustment Programme for Ireland*, Brussels: European Commission, Directorate-General for Economic and Financial Affairs.

13 Central Statistics Office, *Government Finance Statistics (A)*, available from: https://www.cso.ie/en/statistics/governmentaccounts/governmentfinancestatisticsa/

14 Central Statistics Office (2020) *Earnings and Labour Costs Annual Data 2019*, available from: https://www.cso.ie/en/releasesandpublications/er/elca/earningsandlabourcostsannualdata2019/

15 An Oifig Buiséid Pharlaiminteach/Parliamentary Budget Office (2020) *National Debt – An Overview*, April, available from https://data.oireachtas.ie/ie/oireachtas/parliamentaryBudgetOffice/2020/2020-04-21_national-debt-an-overview_en.pdf.

16 Central Banking (2019) 'IMF Sounds Warning over Global Debt', 19 December, available from: https://www.centralbanking.com/node/4615606.

17 Central Bank of Ireland (2019) 'Household Debt Continues to Decline but Remains Fifth Highest in the EU', 23 October, available from: http://www.centralbank.ie/news-media/press-releases/press-release-household-debt-continues-to-decline-but-remains-fifth-highest-in-the-eu-23-october-2019.

18 Central Statistics Office (2020) *Household Finance and Consumption Survey 2018: Debt and Credit*, available from: https://www.cso.ie/en/releasesandpublications/ep/p-hfcs/householdfinanceandconsumptionsurvey2018/debtandcredit/.

19 Central Statistics Office (2020) *Household Finance and Consumption Survey 2018: Saving*, available from: https://www.cso.ie/en/releasesandpublications/ep/p-hfcs/householdfinanceandconsumptionsurvey2018/saving/.

20 Central Statistics Office (2017) *Household Budget Survey 2015–2016: Household Expenditure*, available from: https://www.cso.ie/en/releasesandpublications/ep/p-hbs/hbs20152016/hexp/.

21 Swedrock, T.L., Hyland, A. and Hastrup, J.L. (1999) 'Changes in the Focus of Cigarette Advertisements in the 1950s', *Tobacco Control*, Vol. 8, No. 1, pp. 111–112.

22 Bennett, J. (2020) 'Radioactive Cosmetics', *Cosmetics and Skin*, available from: https://cosmeticsandskin.com/aba/glowing-complexion.php.

23 Reed, A.B. (2011) 'The History of Radiation Use in Medicine', *Journal of Vascular Surgery*, Vol. 53, No. 1 (supplement), pp. 3S–5S.

24 Sweeney, S. (2018) '"The Radium Water Worked Fine until His Jaw Came Off"'. *A Medical Education*, 19 July, available from: https://amedicaleducation.wordpress.com/2018/07/19/the-radium-water-worked-fine-until-his-jaw-came-off/.

25 Winslow, R. (1990) 'The Radium Water Worked Fine Until His Jaw Fell Off', *Wall Street Journal*, 1 August, available from: https://www.scribd.com/document/188172930/The-Radium-Water-Worked-Fine-Until-His-Jaw-Fell-Off.

26 Estrada, M. (2015) 'Radium Dials and Radium Girls', *Stanford University*, 22 March, available from: http://large.stanford.edu/courses/2014/ph241/estrada2/.

27 *Visit Yap*, 'History of Yap', available from: https://www.visityap.com/culture/history-of-yap/.

28 Bordo, M.D., 'Gold Standard', *The Library of Economics and Liberty*, available from: https://www.econlib.org/library/Enc/GoldStandard.html.

29 Kollen Ghizoni, S. (2013) 'Nixon Ends Convertibility of US Dollars to Gold and Announces Wage/Price Controls', *Federal Reserve History*, 22 November, available from: https://www.federalreservehistory.org/essays/gold-convertibility-ends.

30 *US Department of State Archive* (2008) 'The Bretton Woods Conference, 1944', available from: https://2001-2009.state.gov/r/pa/ho/time/wwii/98681.htm.

31 Zhong, R. (2016) 'India to Replace Largest Bank Notes', *Wall Street Journal*, 9 November, available from: https://www.wsj.com/articles/india-to-phase-out-current-500-and-1000-rupee-bank-notes-1478619693.

32 Marawanyika, G. and Wallace, P. (2015) '175 Quadrillion Zimbabwean Dollars Are Now Worth $5', *Bloomberg*, 11 June, available from: https://www.bloomberg.com/news/articles/2015-06-11/zimbabwe-officially-removes-local-currency-from-circulation.

33 Mangudya, J. (2015) 'Press Statement: Demonetization of the Zimbabwe Dollar', Reserve Bank of Zimbabwe, 9 June, available from: https://www.rbz.co.zw/documents/publications/press/demonetisation-press-statement-9-june-2015.pdf.

34 *Central Bank of Ireland*, 'Replace Old or Damaged Money', available from: https://www.centralbank.ie/consumer-hub/notes-and-coins/exchange-of-notes-and-coins.

35 *Citizens Information* (2018) 'About the Euro', available from: https://www.citizensinformation.ie/en/money_and_tax/personal_finance/eu_payments/euro.html.

36 McCray, B. (2006) 'Million vs. Billion vs. Trillion', *Small Biz Survival*, available from: https://smallbizsurvival.com/2006/03/million-vs-billion-vs-trillion.html.